# GRAND CANYON
# LOOP HIKES I

# GRAND CANYON

## Loop Hikes I

**GEORGE STECK**

**Chockstone Press**
Evergreen, Colorado
1989

Published by
Chockstone Press, Inc.
Post Office Box 3505
Evergreen, Colorado 80439

ISBN 0-934641-19-6

# WARNING

More and more often, bodies of hikers and climbers are being found in the adventure setting, including the Grand Canyon, with a guidebook or xeroxed pages thereof in their possession. This coincidence does not mean guidebooks are responsible for these deaths, but it does mean that guidebooks account for increasing use of remote areas where help is a long way off. Hikers travelling alone in the remote Grand Canyon backcountry – what I call the outback – are particularly at risk because even a sprained ankle, a benign injury under ordinary circumstances, can be fatal if it keeps you from needed water.

Park rangers at Grand Canyon expect one or two accidental deaths per year in the outback – usually the result of heatstroke, dehydration, or falling. Obviously, hiking in the outback can be hazardous to your health; this book describes hikes in just these risky places.

The purpose of this book is to facilitate, not to discourage. I have the same purpose in writing it as Goossen did in writing the book with the intriguing title, *Navajo Made Easier* – I want to make it easier for hikers to enjoy the Grand Canyon outback. However, I have the same problem Goossen had; I cannot make it easy. Similarly, I can try to make the hikes safer, but I cannot make them safe.

The hikes described in this book are for experienced Grand Canyon hikers. At least someone in your hiking party should have prior experience hiking in the area. Not only do I assume experience but I also assume you will be in adequate physical condition. Be aware that these hikes are hard. For some newcomers to the Grand Canyon outback who are otherwise experienced backpackers and who may run marathons, these may be the hardest hikes they have ever made.

**Neither the author or publisher assumes responsibilty for any injury that may result from taking any of the treks described in this book. This is a guide book only; once in the outback you are on your own.**

# FOREWORD

I recall a climbing trip with my brother in California's Sierra Nevada on a glorious sun-drenched day. We had left the Vogelsang High Sierra Camp before dawn, heading toward a snowfilled cirque leading to the summit of Mt. Simmons. Pausing there for a brief rest, we considered the remaining portion of our goal: the thin crest of the Sierra, over 12,000 feet now, leading over to a ridge that rose steeply to the summit of Mt. Maclure nearly a mile to the east. It seemed feasible and we managed to get to the top. Still not content, we ascended Mt. Lyell and then found our way down into Lyell Canyon, back to Vogelsang and into the waiting arms of worried parents at day's end. We were unaware that we had made the first ascent of the class 4, western ridge of Maclure; we knew nothing about climbing, about ropes, pitons and the lore of mountaineering, for we were teenagers. It was 1942: I was 16, my brother was nearing 18.

After the war, our avocations took different directions: I became a mountaineer, journeying to distant mountain ranges of the world to indulge in my passion, while my brother, after moving to Albuquerque to take a position as a research statistician at Sandia National Laboratories, practiced his on the trails, and ultimately in the "outback", the trackless inner regions of the Grand Canyon. However, the circle would close, when George, after an accumulation of some 500 days of mostly off-trail hiking in the Canyon over a period of fifteen years, invited me to join one of his treks. I was fascinated at once by the grandeur, the revelations of light and color, of this remarkable place.

In September of 1982, I was again in the Canyon, this time with George and his friend, Robert Benson (others joined us along the way), for a mindbending, 80-day ordeal-by-rubble walk from Lee's Ferry to Grand Wash Cliffs at Lake Mead. We followed along the northern side of the Colorado River, George's ingenious route permitting us to spend 52 nights camped by the river itself. His planning was meticulous, flawless. The requirements of the Park Service necessitated the preparation of an itinerary (which included the placement of 11 caches) that we eventually followed with excruciating precision. Various elements of this imaginative itinerary were the direct result of original explorations by George and his friends (the Tonto route around Powell Plateau in 1981, and the ascent of 150 Mile Canyon in 1982, for example), and by Harvey Butchart and others in earlier years.

*Grand Canyon Loop Hikes I* is a logical outgrowth of these experiences and represents the first time an author has described off-trail Canyon routes from the North Rim that begin and end at the same roadhead, thus avoiding troublesome car shuttles. Terse descriptions of a significant portion of these routes appear in Harvey Butchart's writings between 1970 and 1984. However, it remained for George to explore them himself and then "loop" them together in a logical sequence.

George presents the four loop hikes (there are others to appear in *Grand Canyon Loop Hikes II and III*) in a precise, readable fashion. He often intersperses basic route descriptions with personal anecdotes and relevant historical material. If you assimilate the detailed information on caveats in Chapter I, there should be little reason not to complete one of these loop hikes.

Having thrashed my way along all of George's routes, endured major (and minor) routefinding indignities and savored the immense visual joy of being in the inner canyon, I can affirm that all of them are worthy objectives. But, were I to choose one to be the more beautiful, it would be the Tapeats/Kanab loop. It connects, as George writes, three of the "must see" places in the Canyon: Deer Creek, Tapeats Creek with Thunder River, and Kanab Canyon. When you leave the roadhead at Indian Hollow, following the trail toward the nearby rim, you are about to encounter that most exquisite of all Canyon vistas: you exit the pinon forest, and suddenly, in the passage of a single second, the immensity of the Grand Canyon appears before you, inviting you to enter and explore its hidden mysteries.

Allen Steck
Berkeley, California
April 1988

# DEDICATION

To the memory of my friend and hiking companion
Robert Benson Eschka
1956-1984

Robert (aka Robert Benson) was an illegal alien from Germany who, torn between love of the Grand Canyon and love of home and family, chose death. After discovering the Grand Canyon in 1975, Robert spent at least six months a year for the next eight years in canyon country. In 1982 he hiked on river right from near Green River, Utah to Pearce Ferry, Arizona, and in 1983 he hiked on river left from Pearce Ferry, Arizona to Moab, Utah. During his explorations, he pioneered many new routes, including an especially exciting one along the Muav ledges from Kanab Creek to Tuckup Canyon.

Er weidet mich auf einer grünen Aue,
und führet mich zum frischen Wasser.

# ACKNOWLEDGEMENTS

It is a pleasure to acknowledge the enormous debt I owe to friends with whom I have shared the many journeys into the Grand Canyon outback that have resulted in the information presented in these pages. In particular, in reverse alphabetical order, I want to recognize the contributions of: my wife, Helen Steck, and our children, Stan, Ricia and Mike; my brother, Allen Steck, and his children, Sara and Lee; and friends, Don and Adair Peterson, Don Mattox, Alice and Bill Kleyboecker, Jim Hickerson, Royce Fletcher and Robert Benson.

I also wish to acknowledge a debt to the Great Facilitators – the staff of the Backcountry Reservation Office who have, over almost two decades, been uniformly friendly and helpful. Among these, I need to single out Tom Davison, Mark Sinclair and Ken Phillips.

Finally, I must give special thanks to those who read early drafts of this manuscript with a critical eye. Any author who has friends that will tell him that his precious offspring has four ears, three eyes and a purple goatee and what to do about it is a very lucky author, indeed. So, special thanks to: Helen, Stan, Al, Mike E., Don M., and Ken.

# CONTENTS

# INTRODUCTION

Welcome to the pleasures of hiking in the rugged and remote areas of Grand Canyon National Park where there are no named trails or routes. Ignoring that part of the Park with named trails eliminates at one stroke many popular segments of the backcounty – for example, the Nankoweap and Tapeats Use Areas, which contain the Tilted Mesa and Thunder River trails, respectively. For obvious reasons, it also eliminates almost all of the Park south of the Colorado River and upstream of Elves Chasm. It might seem that very little is left, but that is not the case. Most of the Wild Use Areas and some of the Primitive ones still remain. I estimate the area of this off-trail, inner canyon backcountry – which I will call simply "the outback" – as 1,000 square miles. This is just over half the area of the Park.

Although the outback is enormous, it is largely unvisited. The Park has about three million visitors per year and a typical one stays only a few hours. In 1987, the outback had just under 900 visitors and a typical one stayed several days. This is very close to one outback visitor per square mile per year.

If the outback were always filled to the capacity permitted under current Backcountry Management Plan rules, there could be over 500 campers there every night. These user nights would probably represent about 50,000 people per year, fifty times more than the 1,000, if that, who are actually there.

I have often wondered why the outback is so underutilized. Do misconceptions frighten possible users away? Is there a lack of information about this part of the Park? Are modern cars unable to get to the roadheads? Is it because foreign visitors don't have the time and domestic ones don't have the interest?

Some of my friends argue that it is lack of information. They feel that the wealth of outback hiking information in Harvey Butchart's books, *Grand Canyon Treks,* and *Grand Canyon Treks II & III* is too cryptic for the average hiker. But I disagree. I think the information is there and only appears "too cryptic" because apprehension, spawned by misconception, leads many readers to approach Dr. Butchart's terse and economical style with trepidation instead of confidence.

My view is that, in spite of ample information, potential users are frightened away; that the outback is perceived as inaccessible and hostile and hiking there as so hazardous and painfully difficult that off-trail hikes are, in the words of an eloquent friend and one-time companion, "...not to be enjoyed but to be endured." There is, of course, some truth to this – certainly some of the roadheads are almost inaccessible and the hikes are strenuous. But, to a large extent, hazard, hostility and struggle are like beauty – they are "in the eye of the beholder."

In this book, I try to present a more balanced view of the outback – to show that for the prepared and experienced hiker it is a place that is both friendly and fun and that hikes there, while strenuous, are not "killer hikes" to be undertaken only by Superhiker.

This book describes four hikes off the North Rim, each approximately a week in duration, which end where they begin. I call them "loop hikes." Taken together they cover the Canyon from Bright Angel Creek on the east to Kanab Creek on the west. Dedicated and energetic hikers with several weeks to spend can even, with the help of caches near rim access points, string these loops together into an extended roundtrip excursion from Phantom Ranch.

Unless you have already hiked in the Grand Canyon, these hikes may be the most physically and mentally demanding ones you have ever taken. This is not an elitist statement; it is the collective opinion of those who have been with me on their first Grand Canyon hike. But in spite of that assessment, I think any hiker in good condition who is comfortable with off-trail travel can do them. But I urge you to hike with at least one companion who has had experience with off-trail hiking in the Grand Canyon. Although I have tried to be sufficiently detailed in my route descriptions to keep you on course, some outback route finding experience may still be required. But, more importantly, I feel it is critical for at least one member of any hiking group to have had Grand Canyon experience in dealing with heat. Failure to deal with it properly causes more problems throughout the Grand Canyon than anything else.

There is an enormous amount of rugged and remote Canyon to be enjoyed and I hope that the hikes I describe here will help you participate in its enjoyment.

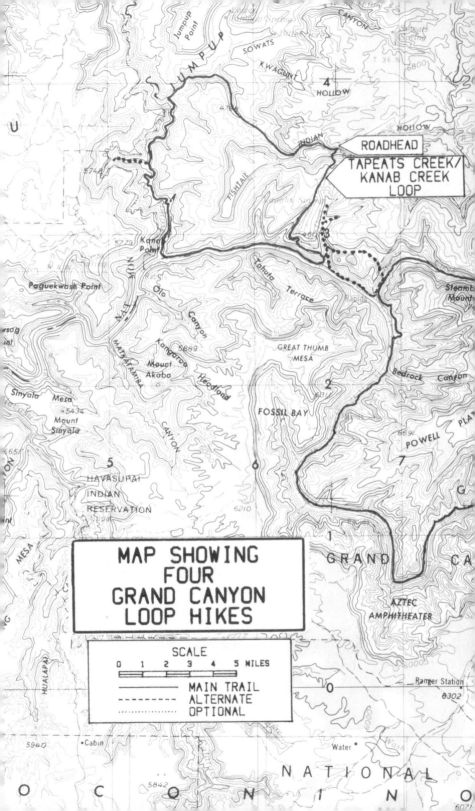

ROADHEAD
TAPEATS CREEK/
KANAB CREEK
LOOP

MAP SHOWING
FOUR
GRAND CANYON
LOOP HIKES

SCALE

0  1  2  3  4  5 MILES

——————— MAIN TRAIL
- - - - - - - ALTERNATE
·············· OPTIONAL

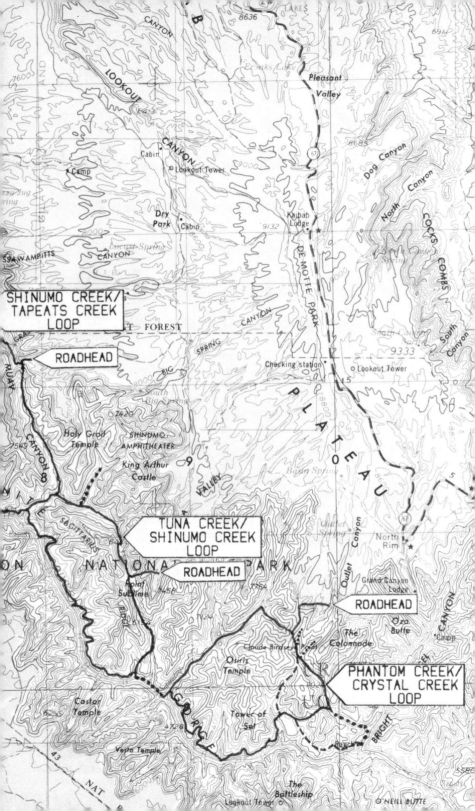

**SHINUMO CREEK/ TAPEATS CREEK LOOP**

**ROADHEAD**

**TUNA CREEK/ SHINUMO CREEK LOOP**

**ROADHEAD**

**ROADHEAD**

**PHANTOM CREEK/ CRYSTAL CREEK LOOP**

# — 1 —

# COMMENTS AND CAVEATS

## (How to Use this Book)

A general statement of condition:
*"Those who die will be the lucky ones."*
author unknown

**PERMITS**  A permit is required for all overnight camping below the rim in Grand Canyon National Park (GCNP). You obtain one by either: (1) going to a Backcountry Reservation Office on either the North or South Rims or (2) sending a permit request to the Backcountry Reservation Office, P.O. Box 129, Grand Canyon, Arizona 86023. Call (602) 638-2474 weekdays 1100-1700 (MST) for information or for the Trip Planning Packet. Permits cannot be obtained over the phone.

**USE AREAS**  The GCNP Backcountry Use Area Map, that comes with the Trip Planning Packet, is useful for preparing your request for a reservation. The backcountry is divided into over 75 Use Areas (79 as of Oct 1987) and each Use Area is allowed only so many parties (1 to 8 people) and/or groups (9 to 16 people) per night. On October 1, reservations can be made for the remainder of that year and for all of the next year. A request for a reservation should give the number of people and list the names of the Use Areas in which you wish to camp each night. Don't forget to request a reservation for nights spent at the roadhead at the beginning or end of a hike.

**BACK PACKING RULES**  Besides the rules you might expect, here are two you might not: i) no cooking fires and no campfires, in other words, no fires, period; and ii) carry out your used toilet paper – it helps to have a plastic bag reserved for this purpose. The second rule prevents the visual pollution of partially buried toilet paper and the two together should prevent a toilet paper fire like the one at Deer Creek which burned several acres and destroyed several big cottonwoods.

Everyone who comes to the Grand Canyon to hike should *MAPS* be familiar with the United States Geological Survey (USGS) 15 minute quadrangle maps – the common topo map – and its aggregation, the GCNP map. It should be noted, however, that this large map, in spite of its seemingly all-encompassing title, includes only a little more than half the Park.

The USGS has either mapped, or is mapping, parts of the *USGS* Grand Canyon to five different scales. These five scales are: *Maps*
1) The 1:62500 maps. These are the 15' topo maps. All of Grand Canyon is mapped to this scale except to the west of 113 degrees of longitude – the west side of the Tuckup Quadrangle.
2) The 1:24000 maps. These are the 7.5' topo maps. They cover Grand Canyon to the west of 113 degrees of longitude and that part of Marble Canyon to the north of 36.5 degrees of latitude – the north side of the Nankoweap Quadrangle. Soon this series will cover the whole Canyon.
3) The 1:100000 maps. These are called the 100K maps or metric maps and, as of October 1987, this is the smallest scale to which the entire Grand Canyon is mapped. They have a contour interval of 50 meters.
4) The 1:250000 maps. Four of these maps will cover all of the Grand Canyon. A raised relief form of these maps is produced and sold by Hubbard, P.O. Box 104, Northbrook, Illinois 60062.
5) The 1:48000 maps. Though these three maps contain information not on later ones, they are mainly of historical interest. Two are the famous East Half and West Half maps of GCNP prepared from surveys done in 1902 and 1923. The latest edition is that of 1927 though it was reprinted as late as 1961. The third map is the Grand Canyon National Monument map. All have a contour interval of 50 feet.

Two more maps, based on USGS maps, are especially useful.

One is "The Geologic Map of the Grand Canyon", also *Fault* affectionately known as the "Fault Map". It is published by *Map* the Grand Canyon Natural History Association and shows what strata can be seen where. It also shows where the faults are. Such a map is important because faults often provide hiking and/or climbing routes through cliff systems that would otherwise be impossible obstacles. Besides these notable virtues it has one that is even more notable – it is an exquisitely beautiful map.

*Plastic Park Map* The other, which first went on sale in 1987, is a modification of the big GCNP map. In effect, the Park map has been cut in half, reduced in size slightly (the new scale is approximately 1:73530 but the contour interval remains 80 feet), and each half printed on opposite sides of a sheet of waterproof, tearproof plastic roughly two by three feet in size. Its title is "Grand Canyon National Park." It is copyrighted by Trails Illustrated and published by Ponderosa Printing Co., P.O. Box 3610, Evergreen, Colorado 80439-3425. Besides being almost indestructible, it has the very useful feature of having the Use Areas outlined in gray. This is a better map for trip planning than the one that comes in the Trip Planning Packet.

*Washburn Map* Other maps deserve honorable mention. One is the 1978 map, "The Heart of the Grand Canyon", published by the National Geographic Society in collaboration with Bradford Washburn at the Boston Museum of Science. A version of it – abbreviated a little in the E-W direction – was an insert in the July, 1978 issue of *National Geographic*. Its scale is 1:2400 and it extends from the Grand Canyon Village on the South Rim to the campground on the North Rim and from Grapevine Creek on the east almost to Crystal Creek on the west. It has 100 foot contours and is shaded.

*3-D Map* Especially deserving of honorable mention are anaglyphic maps. An anaglyphic map is a topographic map with two sets of contours in different colors – one set for each eye. Each contour in a set is displaced by an amount proportional to its elevation – one set displaced to the left for the right eye and one to the right for the left eye. When you look at the map through appropriately colored lenses, you see a remarkably realistic three-dimensional relief map.

One such map, prepared in Germany, appears in the book *Grand Canyon*, by E. A. Heiniger and published in 1975 by Robert B. Luce Co., Inc. It covers about the same area as the National Geographic map at a scale of 1:62500 with 200 foot contours. But what first attracted me to the book were the animal pictures. I marveled at the patience required to get all the ones of coyotes, mountain lions, bobcats, deer, caco-mistles, and so on. Many of the pictures were taken in the neighborhood of the Tuweep Valley, and one time when I was visiting the ranger there, John Riffey, I mentioned my delight at all those animal pictures. He gave me an amused look and said, "I hate to be the one to tell you this, but all those animals were rented from the Tucson Zoo." I don't enjoy the animal pictures as much anymore, but I still greatly admire the map.

Another anaglyphic map of the entire Grand Canyon was published in 1988 by Cygnus Graphic. Order from R.L. Smith, Box 10264, Phoenix, Arizona 85064-0264. The scale is 1:300000 and the contour interval is 400 feet.

I still must mention one final map. This is the Kaibab National *Forest* Forest map (North Kaibab Ranger District) which shows all *Map* the forest roads and their designations. It is a great help in getting to remote roadheads and is available at the Jacob Lake Store (ask the cashier), at the nearby Forest Service trailer, and at the Forest Service Ranger Station in Fredonia, Arizona.

Each route description in this book has an accompanying *ROUTE* map which shows the route with a solid line, alternate *DETAILS* routings with dashed lines and optional day hikes with dotted lines. Possible campsites are shown with small tepees and useful springs and sheltering overhangs are shown with an "S" and "O", respectively. A summary map follows below.

I have decided not to give an index of loop difficulty because *LOOP* all the loops are difficult in one way or another. Moreover, *DIFFICULTY* difficulties are sometimes in the eyes of the beholder and can depend on variables like weather or river flow. Besides, a hike is often easier the second time you make it than it was the first. I intend, though, to mention objective difficul-ties, like long days away from water, when the occasion arises.

A table of hiking times between segments of a loop is given *HIKING* for each loop. I have chosen to give these times, which *TIMES* include reststops but not lunch and which are rounded to the nearest fifteen minutes, rather than distances because I consider them more informative. There are some places in the Canyon where it may take me two and a half hours to go a mile and there are others where I can zip along a burro trail and do a mile in 20 minutes. So, if I'm heading to water,

I feel it is more important to know how far away it is in time than how far away it is in miles. If I need them, I can estimate distances from a map.

I was in my late 50's before I began collecting routes and hiking times and thought of writing a book such as this and although I have slowed down in recent years, I still think the times I give are average for an experienced off-trail Grand Canyon hiker in good condition. Some can certainly go a good deal faster and some will want to go slower, but remember that a group travels only as fast as its slowest member. To calibrate yourself, I suggest a preliminary comparison of your times to mine and adjusting mine accordingly.

*CAMPSITES* Some of the locations in the Hiking Times table are good campsites. They are designated by the "tepee" symbol, **Δ**. The appropriate Use Area name is shown alongside each tepee to help in the preparation of your request for a permit.

*GRAND* Bill Hall, Boucher, Bright Angel, Hermit, Horsethief, North
*CANYON* Bass, Old Hance, Thunder River, Tilted Mesa – these are
*TRAILS* some of the names given to Canyon trails. Collectively, they evoke memories – some tragic – of other times and the people who lived them. Bill Hall, for example, was a young North Rim ranger who was killed in 1979 in one car wreck while enroute to another. But history is only one aspect of the concept of trail. Except for the Bright Angel and the North and South Kaibab Trails, which are the only ones routinely maintained, all the named trails are either rarely maintained, unmaintained or abandoned. According to a 1984 NPS News Release, there are 30.7 miles of maintained trails and over 400 miles of all the other kinds.

*What* What else is a trail? The word connotes a certain ease of
*is a* travel. But there is a great difference between hiking on the
*Trail?* Bright Angel Trail and hiking on the Horsethief Trail. The first is a Canyon equivalent of Interstate 40 complete with flashy sportscars, convoys of semis and even an occasional smokey. The second, after almost one hundred years of abandonment, is only a route marked by a few horseshoes, a few pans, a coffeepot and the rusted out skeletons of a few tin cans. So, the concept of "trail" has both interest and relevance.

*The* For the most part, the "trails" taking you off the North Rim
*Trail* to the edge of what I have called "The Outback" are either
*as* historical artifacts or game trails. The first trails into the
*History* Canyon were game trails, and when the ancient inhabitants

of the Canyon began using them, they made some modest improvements – like leaning a log against a cliff or piling up stones at a useful spot. But I doubt that much else was done. Neither bare feet, nor even feet with mocassins, could scuff out much of a trail bed. That would come later when prospectors, miners, and cowboys ventured into the area.

Most of the named trails which exist today as something more than just a route were built by miners to get their ore to the rim and by cowboys to get their stock to good grazing. The remnants of their constructed trails into the Canyon abound and are silent witness to the enormous amounts of time and energy these people had. The North Bass Trail, when you can find it, is such a testimonial. Besides the Horsethief Trail, whose users probably didn't have much time for construction, cowboys built several trails into the area west of Kanab Creek. Few are in good enough condition for hikers today let alone cattle or horses.

One interesting sidelight of "the trail as history" is "the trail as property". Mining laws of the Old West gave a miner sole rights to the use of any trail he built to his mine. When the railroad began bringing tourists to Grand Canyon in 1901, "ownership" of trails became a better source of income than the mines they served. Pete Berry recorded his trail to a small mine at Indian Garden as a toll road in 1891. This was a predecessor to the now-familiar Bright Angel Trail. Berry extended the trail to the river in 1899 by a route quite different from the current one. *The Trail As Property*

After Berry received a five year extension of his Bright Angel Trail rights, Ralph Cameron bought him out. This was 1901, the year the railroad arrived, and there was money to be made. The fee charged for using this "Old" Bright Angel Trail was one dollar per head, and by 1915 Cameron was "mining" the trail for $20,000 per year. But he did very little to maintain it and various agencies who, in turn, had jurisdiction over the South Rim area resented Cameron's exploitation and sought remedy in the courts – to no avail. The battle was still being waged in 1919 when the National Park Service assumed jurisdiction.

Cameron was elected to the U.S. Senate in 1920, and, in 1922, got a measure of revenge by having operating funds for Grand Canyon National Park eliminated from the Interior Department appropriation. Also in 1922, possibly seeking some revenge of its own, the Park Service began building the South Kaibab Trail to compete with Cameron's trail. I think Coconino County had Cameron's rights by then, but such was Cameron's political power that he was still collecting his one dollar per head. In 1925 The Kaibab Trail was finished, in 1926 Cameron lost his bid for reelection and on May 22, 1928 the Park Service finally acquired the long-sought deed to the Old Bright Angel Trail.

*Game Trails*  The most extensive network of trails in the Canyon today has been created by animals – deer, mountain sheep and, until they were eradicated(?), burros. Always be on the lookout for game trails – they often appear when you most need them. When you find one, you will discover that even the skimpiest can sometimes double your speed – especially in the difficult places. Not only do they give you something a little flatter to walk on, but they also give you steadier footing. Their effect is so dramatic that I have often been led to speculate about a mathematical definition of "trail." I haven't anything worldshaking to offer, but I do know the concept involves more than just the area around your feet.

*The Trail As Minimum Energy Trajectory*  Often in following a deer trail, I find it goes up steeply and over a high "pass" when I would just as soon keep contouring. Deer aren't stupid, so why this seemingly unnecessary work? I think the answer is that it actually takes less energy to go up and over and back down than it does to go all the way around. I call such trails "minimum energy trajectories." The notion is important. In contouring around, one is inevitably faced with the dilemma of whether to contour in to the head of a drainage and then back out or to climb down to the bed and then back up. Ninety five percent of the time I go down and then back up. The rest of the time I don't and wish I had.

*This is a Trail*  So, what is a trail? Basically, a trail is a track that gets you from one place to another more easily than if it weren't there. All trails were probably game trails originally. Some, like the Bright Angel Trail, became an Indian trail and then a major Park highway. Some, like the South Bass, Tanner and Old Hance Trails, were built by miners to move ore. Some, like the Tuckup and Horsethief Trails, were built by cowboys to move stock. Some, like the North Bass Trail, were built by entrepreneurs in the tourist business to move dudes.

All now move hikers and some, in fact, are being maintained by hikers. Twenty years ago the Tilted Mesa Trail was barely even a route and was hard to follow. Now it is a fairly good trail and is easy to follow. More and more, the abandoned trails are being resurrected by increasing use as more and more hikers use them for access to increasingly distant places.

It is instructive as well as helpful to know the sequence of *GEOLOGY* strata. In what follows, the structure designations are C = cliff, L = ledge, S = slope. Structure is important – cliffs usually mean trouble, ledges sometimes mean shelter, and slopes always mean easy route finding.

| STRATUM | COLOR | HT. (ft.) | AGE (M yrs) | STRUC-TURE | | |
|---|---|---|---|---|---|---|
| Kaibab Limestone | grayish white | 300 | 250 | C | | |
| Toroweap Limestone | grayish white | 200 | 260 | C | L | |
| Coconino Sandstone | creamy white | 300 | 270 | C | | |
| Hermit Shale | deep red | 300 | 280 | | | S |
| Supai Group | deep red | 600 | 300 | C | L | S |
| Redwall Limestone | gray stained red | 600 | 330 | C | | |
| Muav Limestone | gray with yellow | 500 | 530 | C | L | |
| Bright Angel Shale | blue green | 300 | 540 | | | S |
| Tapeats Sandstone | dark brown | 100 | 550 | C | L | |
| Vishnu Schist | black with mica | 1,200 | 2,000 | | L | S |

Other less common formations are also of interest to hikers. These are members of the Grand Canyon Supergroup which are between the Tapeats and the schist in age. They are the oldest sedimentary rocks in the Canyon and from the top down the ones to which I will want to refer are:

| STRATUM | COLOR | HT. (ft.) | AGE (M yrs) | STRUC-TURE | | |
|---|---|---|---|---|---|---|
| Dox Sandstone | red,purple,brown | 2,000 | >1100 | | | S |
| Shinumo Quartzite | red,purple,white | 1,200 | >1100 | C | | |
| Hakatai Shale | reddish orange | 800 | >1100 | | | S |
| Bass Formation | grayish green (columnar jointing) | 250 | >1100 | C | L | |

A backcountry ranger once taught me the memory aid, "Know The Canyon's History. Study Rocks Made By Time", to order the strata from top to bottom. You must add the "V" for Vishnu yourself. Creating your own sentences may help you remember the order better. For example, "Kick The Can Hard. Some Rogue May Bring Along The Vodka." If you keep track of the strata, you can notice, for example, that the Bright Angel Shale and the Tapeats are going under water as you go downstream from Deer Creek toward Kanab Creek. This is bad news because hiking on the Tapeats is usually fairly easy.

The dark rocks of the Vishnu Schist are the roots of ancient mountains that geologists think may have been 20,000 feet high. After a billion years these mountains were worn down flat and the Grand Canyon Supergroup and later the Tapeats laid down on top of them.

*Tonto*  The Tonto Platform – or just Tonto – is the plateau on top of the Tapeats. The line of contact between the Tapeats and the Schist is called The Great Unconformity and it is hard to believe a billion years of geology has been there and vanished.

*Supai*  As you might guess from the structure of the Supai, it is composed of sandstones, limestones, and shales. The three main cliffs are sandstones, the slopes are shales, and scattered through it all are layers of limestone.

*Coconino*  The Coconino is an aeolian formation – a petrified sand dune. You can see the layering of the windblown sand and how some layers meet others at an angle.

*Oceans*  Oceans have come and gone many times over the area known *and*  as Grand Canyon. Imagine the ocean deepening over a point *Strata*  on an ancient shoreline – the word is "transgression." The *Deposition*  first thing to accumulate there is sand. Whether windblown or waterborne, it is too heavy to be carried out to sea and collects as a sediment. Next, as the water deepens at our location, the finer silts that are carried out to sea begin to collect. Finally, in deeper water yet, limestones precipitate out and settle to the bottom. When an ocean withdraws from an area, this time the word is "regression", the process of deposition is reversed.

According to Collier's book (see Bibliography), limestones form at the rate of 400 ft/M yrs; shales at the rate of 2,000 ft/M yrs; and sandstones at the rate of 1,000 ft/M yrs. Thus, deposition of 600 feet of Redwall would take about 1.5 million years and 100 feet of Tapeats about 100,000 years. So all the sedimentary deposits were laid down in about five million years. Since the Tapeats is about 500 million years old, it would appear that the Grand Canyon region was above water for 99 percent of the last 500 million years.

Something else occurred to me only when I read of it in *Pangea*
Redfern's book (see Bibliography). Because the breakup of
the supercontinent Pangea began about 200 million years ago
and because the youngest stratum is older than that, it
follows that all the Canyon strata were laid down before the
breakup. When you look at the Canyon you are seeing a
groove in a piece of an ancient supercontinent that broke off
and drifted a great distance. But remember that the grooving
is recent. It took about five million years beginning about
ten million years ago.

Spring and Fall are both good times for hiking in the Canyon *THE*
but I prefer Fall because the weather is more stable. In early *INNER*
Spring (March/April) it can seem to be boiling one day and *CANYON*
freezing the next. In fact, I remember one Easter when we *IS HOT*
fried one day and had a blizzard the next.

TEMPERATURES (°F) AND RAINFALL (inches)
AT PHANTOM RANCH

|  | J | F | M | A | M | J | J | A | S | O | N | D |
|---|---|---|---|---|---|---|---|---|---|---|---|---|
| Maximum | 72 | 82 | 88 | 98 | 109 | 114 | 119 | 120 | 108 | 102 | 84 | 70 |
| Ave. Max. | 56 | 62 | 71 | 82 | 92 | 101 | 106 | 103 | 97 | 84 | 68 | 57 |
| Ave. Min. | 36 | 42 | 48 | 56 | 63 | 72 | 78 | 75 | 69 | 58 | 46 | 37 |
| Minimum | 26 | 31 | 32 | 27 | 46 | 61 | 62 | 59 | 49 | 41 | 31 | 30 |
| Ave. Rainfall | .7 | .8 | .8 | .5 | .4 | .3 | .8 | 1.4 | 1.0 | .7 | .4 | .9 |

The source for the averages is *Information for running the
Colorado River through the Grand Canyon,* a booklet published
by the National Park Service at Grand Canyon. The span of
time determining the averages is not given. The extremes
were extracted by the author from Phantom Ranch daily
temperature records for the years 1980-87. One curiosity
emerged. These daily records for August showed several
highs of 120 degrees F, but no higher one – six highs of 120
seemed to me much less likely than, say, five of 120 and one
of 121. When I humorously remarked to the custodian of the
data that the abundance of readings of 120 showed a pref-
erence for nice round numbers on the part of the data
collector, I was told, "Oh no, it doesn't mean that at all, it's
just that the old thermometer only went to 120." This
deficiency was remedied in 1986 and Phantom Ranch can
now register a high of 135 when it needs to.

*CRITTERS*  Hikers in the Grand Canyon should expect to interact with several species of animals. The ones I will comment on specifically are: rattlesnakes, scorpions, mice, ringtails, ravens and ants.

*Rattle*  First, I must say that any rattlesnake bite is potentially life
*snakes*  threatening and I advise any Grand Canyon hiker to decide beforehand what he or she will do should a rattlesnake bite occur. Second, I must add that my experience over many years of Canyon hiking shows the risk of a rattlesnake bite to be small; in fact, I have no personal knowledge of anyone being bitten in the Grand Canyon. Third, I have concluded that a rattlesnake bite is rarely fatal to a healthy adult.

This view is supported by the following data – of the 19 deaths from snakebite reported in New Mexico over the years 1931-1972 (Amerindian deaths from snakebite were not reported), 14 were 10 years old or younger and three were 70 or older. This means only about ten percent of the fatalities were were between ten and 70 years of age. Further, in October, 1987 the *Albuquerque Journal* had an article on snakebite which said there are about 7,000 venomous snakebites per year in the United States, with an average of 20 deaths per year; another reference adds that most of the dead are children.

Grand Canyon rattlesnakes are said to be "rare and retiring." I'm not sure what that means but I expect to see one or two during a week's trip – although I once saw ten in one day. A snake may rattle if you come on it when it is warm, but in the cool of early morning they often don't. At such a time all the hikers in my group may file past a rattlesnake and only one person sees it. I hate to think how often this happens and nobody sees it.

I remember once having a related problem. I stepped up on a rock that almost shook with the combined buzzing of several snakes. Being, at the time, deaf in one ear, I had no directional hearing and could not tell where the snakes were. ⁚     ⁚se to remain on top of the rock until someone came  \     :ould tell. There were four snakes under the rock and a  ₊ ..otograph showed one had at least 16 rattles.

*Snakebite*  Granting that the risk of being bitten is small, what do you
*Treatment*  do if, against all odds, you are bitten? First, you observe that even if you are bitten, there is a one in five chance that the snake did not inject any venom – remember venom is primarily for getting food and not for defense. So 20 percent

of the time you have to do nothing. The rest of the time do as recommended below.

A short article in *Parade Magazine* for August 12, 1984 describes what Dr. Willis Wingert, a USC professor of pediatrics and emergency medicine, considers appropriate treatment for snakebite. I wrote Dr. Wingert and asked what he would recommend for a rattlesnake bite in the backcountry of the Grand Canyon where it might be several days before a victim could get help. He replied as follows.

"My advice for a person who is in a remote area and is bitten by a rattlesnake is to remain quiet, splint the bitten extremity (stick and cloth or a pillow splint), drink large quantities of any fluid except alcohol, and send a companion to hike out for helicopter rescue. Cutting, sucking, tourniquets and freezing will not prevent the absorption of venom. It is doubtful that sucking could remove any significant amount of venom. These methods only complicate the problem by damaging tissue (which already is poisoned), introducing infection into the wound and possibly causing severe hemorrhage. A snakebitten victim doesn't need these additional problems. I reassure you that you have hours to get help. Of course, the sooner treatment is started the better but even severely bitten victims survive 24 to 48 hours." *Be Quiet* *Use Splint* *Take Water* *Get Help*

Dr. Wingert also went on to recommend hiking with a walking stick for probing ahead so that your stick "finds" the snake before your leg does. I appreciated that suggestion because I've always used one, but his recommendation against the use of tourniquets surprised me. However, an article "New Light on Snakebite" by Nelson Wadsworth in *Outdoor Life*, March, 1969, described experiments by a Florida doctor who used radioactive venom on dogs and found that 80 percent of the venom was still at the injection site after two hours. This suggests that diffusion of venom may already be slow enough without a tourniquet, especially since attendant swelling also slows the circulation.

Dr. Wingert's suggestion to send a companion for help should be expanded to include the use of a signal mirror. My two personal experiences show signal mirrors to be supremely effective but I have a friend who has had her own experiences and does not share my optimistic view. I still recommend their use. *Signal Mirror*

*Electric Shock* Over the years I have collected about 20 references dealing with rattlesnake bites and have noticed fads come and go. In the early 60s ice bags were a comer – now they are a goner. The most recent comer uses a modified stun gun (*Time*, August 18, 1987, page 58 and, more recently, *Outdoor Life*, June, 1988, page 65 and July, 1988, page 45). If this treatment survives, it will be the simplest of all. As of the moment, however, if I am envenomated, I will follow Dr. Wingert's advice AND use a signal mirror.

*Why Not Antivenin?* With all the discussion of what to do for snakebite, why was nothing said about antivenin? There are several reasons it is not recommended for use by backpackers. One, it is itself hazardous and should be administered only in the hospital or clinic setting by health professionals. Two, it needs to be kept cold to maintain its potency and may not last long in the Grand Canyon. Finally, it is expensive – over $100/vial – and proper treatment may require more than one vial.

*Tissue Necrosis* I will close my discussion of rattlesnakes on a somber note. Even if we agree that rattlesnake bites are rarely fatal, I must remind you that their venom is a poison which destroys tissue. This means that although you probably won't die you might lose a few fingers or toes or possibly a limb.

When the venom causes swelling, the muscle swells within its sheath and the blood vessels within the muscle are constricted as if with an internal tourniquet. Gangrene may result.

It is with the idea of minimizing loss of tissue that I offer the following heroic measure in the event worst has come to worst. If it has been several days since the bite, if your leg is badly swollen and your toes are turning black and if rescue is still problematical, then I suggest you consider taking a razor blade and slitting the muscle sheath. This should reduce the effect of the swelling in cutting off circulation.

*Scorpions* While no companion of mine has been bitten by a snake, I have had two companions stung by scorpions. Scorpions hunt at night and don't usually wander around during the day. For some sobering excitement try hiking at night with an ultraviolet light – scorpions fluoresce under UV light. Watch out, though, when a hard rain floods their hiding places and they come out in great numbers. We counted over twenty scorpions in a very small area after such a rain. A companion, walking barefoot over the slab rock, stepped on one of these. This became a serious medical emergency when the young lady developed a severely depressed respiratory reflex and had to be evacuated. She almost died of that scorpion sting.

My nephew, on the other hand, was stung on the elbow and only had numbness, preceded by a tingling sensation, travel up his arm. He was sure he would die when that numbness reached his heart but, fortunately, he fell asleep before that happened. His pulse and respiration remained good through the night and by morning he was okay except his arm was "all a-tingle."

My advice about scorpions: "wear shoes at night and after a rain, and be careful about turning over rocks."

*Ringtails* Ringtailed cats, more accurately called "cacomistles", are a frequent pest – particularly at Deer Creek. They are nocturnal, omnivorous and fearless. A friend took a flash picture of one fighting over possession of his pack and my nephew made a mistake trying to pull one out of his pack by the tail. They are also strong – able to carry off pound loaves of pumpernickel. They scamper around on cliff faces and make a chittering noise somewhat like that of a chipmunk. But I think they have a problem with overhangs; so hang up your food under one, but far enough from the wall so they can't reach it.

*Ravens* According to Scandinavian mythology, when Odin sits on his throne, the ravens Hugin and Munin, representing thought and memory, sit on his shoulders. Every day they fly over the whole world and report back on what they have seen. As a result, ravens are sometimes called "the eyes of Odin."

I always have enjoyed watching ravens. I think the reason is that they almost always seem to be in pairs, and I like thinking that an intelligent bird like the raven can desire and appreciate companionship. I once watched a pair of ravens engaged in a variety of acrobatics – I particularly remember their climbing high and then diving – and I couldn't help feeling this was play and they were having fun. Unfortunately, these thoughts are probably only anthropomorphisms on a grand scale.

*Ravens as Pests* But ravens can also be pests. A pair watched us at Deer Creek one morning as we were breakfasting and I thought I had better protect my pack before we took off on a day hike. I closed the pockets and tied down the straps and put it on its back in a small space under an overhang. When we returned I found someone or something had pulled open the zippers and scattered the contents of the pockets. I have to admit I did not see the ravens do this, but nothing was stolen except edibles. Mice couldn't do it and ringtails probably couldn't. But ravens have the intelligence and the dexterity to do it and I'm sure they did. So enjoy the ravens but be wary.

*Mice* I have a stressful relationship with mice. They are almost everywhere in the canyon, and there are very smart mice at some places. At least I used to think so until I was told that what I took for intelligence was just instinct. The foraging habits of the genus *Peromyscus* take them up trees and out branches and down whatever they find there. Thus instinct and not learned response has led them to climb down the cord I use to suspend my food. But what is it that leads them to gnaw through the cord dropping the food to the ground? Luck? My son claims this has happened to him.

*The* I have spent considerable time and energy trying to best the
*Mouse* lowly mouse and at the moment it is "Mice 513 and Steck 0."
*as* One night I thought I would surely outwit them if I balanced
*Adversary* my bags of food on the top of my aluminum alloy skipole walking stick. I awoke during the night and saw my food outlined against the moonlit sky and thought smugly, "At last, I've outwitted them this time." Then I noticed a small bump on top of the food, but I don't see very well at night without my glasses and I didn't pay any attention until the bump moved. Unfortunately, the human eye is especially designed to detect movement and I couldn't very well ignore it. I sat up quickly and the bump ran down my skipole. Not "carefully climbed" down the skipole, but "ran" down – headfirst. I had suddenly been transformed from the outwitter to the outwittee.

For the next few minutes I watched many mice run up and down my skipole many times. I found out in the morning that mice are also very picky eaters. They ate everything out of my bags of mixed nuts except the peanuts.

At the moment I have only one surefire way of keeping my food for my own use – I put it in a pot, put the lid on and weigh it down with stones.

But I still have hopes of outwitting them. As an experiment I once bought some stainless steel screening – like window screen but made of stainless steel. I assumed that mice, and maybe even rock squirrels and ringtails, couldn't chew through it. I cut a piece about a foot on a side and put all kinds of goodies on it – nuts, chunks of granola, raisins, M and M's. Then I folded the screen over and stapled the sides together. I took this purse of tasty tidbits with me on a trip to Hermit Camp and left it out during the night.

The next morning I found tooth marks all over the thing but the contents were intact. I found pleasure in the thought of all the frustration I had created and thought I would leave it out the next night, too. That was a mistake; the rock squirrels took it to the shop for further study. I only hope that to this day their nest is filled with delicious but unattainable aromas. I think the experiment was a success, but I have not yet made a stainless steel screen liner with metal zipper closures for my backpack – just lazy, I guess. Or perhaps I'm afraid something big will haul my pack off to the shop for further study.

I have two other ideas to use when the need arises. The first is to slip a eight-inch section of stainless steel tubing onto the skipole. I don't think a mouse can run up stainless steel. The second is to take my 10-inch pot lid and drill an eighth inch hole in the center. Then I feed one end of a six-foot piece of nylon cord with a knot in the middle through the hole. When I tie that end to a branch and tie my food to the other, I have the food suspended below a lid. Any mouse coming down the cord to the lid and walking out on it will tip the lid sending the marauder tumbling to the ground. Cynics say I will send the mouse tumbling down on my food. Ha! What do they know?

If none of these ideas work, I still have another one. I will put out a small dish of Everclear during the night. The next morning I can pick up the comatose bodies and dispose of them in any way I see fit at the time.

Finally, I want to add something about ants. I don't worry *Ants* much about ants. It is hard to get rid of the tiny black ones once they invade your pack but they are more an aesthetic pain than anything else. And the red ones, with the bite you can't soon forget, have the happy habit of going to bed when it gets dark. Still, ants are interesting.

I studied these red ants at length one time when I had *Ants* hundreds of maggots to dispose of. I was on my through- *Versus* Canyon hike and had just retrieved a cache I had hidden *Larvae* along Tapeats Creek. Through a tactical error committed at home while packing the food containers, I had allowed moths to contaminate them and when the cache was opened it was crawling with moth larvae. I was uncivilized enough to want revenge and I picked the larvae out of the food and put them by a nearby anthill. The ants quickly swarmed over them and, one by one, hauled the wriggly things below ground.

It was apparently a mixed blessing because several hours later I glanced at the anthill and saw larvae scattered about. As I watched, more were hauled out. They were still alive though somewhat subdued. I can only guess what went on underground. Did the larvae thrash about too much and begin breaking up the furniture? Did the larvae fight back and bite off a few ant legs? Did the ants eat one and find it tasted terrible? I'll never know, but I am still curious.

On another afternoon, I gave some ants a large peanut. With great industry and greater stupidity, they moved it to the edge of the clearing where their hole was. To my delight the peanut got away from its handlers and rolled down on the hole, blocking it completely. I watched that anthill closely as the afternoon passed to see what the final outcome might be. Then it was margarita time, and then it was dinner time, so it was almost dark before I took another look.

To my surprise both the peanut and the ant hole were gone. There was still a bare patch of ground, though it seemed less bare than before, but there was no hole. All I saw were five ants moving a few small stones around, seemingly at random. A little later they, too, were gone. Rising especially early the next morning, I found the five ants were back and beginning to open the hole. In about an hour the colony was functioning normally again. It would seem that when red ants go to bed, they pull their hole in after them.

*Agave* While rattlesnakes and scorpions are potentially a serious *Spines* threat, they are not high on my list of dangers. What is highest is not even animal; it is vegetable. The agave cactus has done more harm to me and my friends than any other living thing in the Canyon.

Every time a person stumbles he unconsciously throws out an arm to catch or steady himself. Most of the time nothing serious happens but every once in a while he flings his hand onto an agave spine which enters deeply and breaks off. Surgery is usually required to get it out.

I once had to abort a trip when a five-eighths inch piece broke off in my hand. It had gone into a tendon and I couldn't move my fingers. I might have saved the trip – and $800 – if I had remembered the small pair of pliers I have in the cookkit for stove repairs. There was a chance I could have grabbed the end of the spine with them.

Two other friends have scars on their hands from similar experiences; so beware the agave. It has beautiful blossoms and very sharp teeth.

*Cactus Spines*

I use scissors and tweezers more often than I use a knife. The tweezers are for medium sized cactus spines. Big ones you can get a hold on are pulled out with your fingers and small fuzzy ones are pulled off with adhesive tape.

*Cholla Problems*

In western Grand Canyon the Teddy Bear Cholla is a common problem. On rare occasions the ordinary cholla poses a similar problem elsewhere. Thumbsized segments of cholla cover the ground in some places and every once in a while your boot will pick up one on the inside of the sole as the foot is planted. When the boot moves forward the cholla can transfer from the sole to your leg. The spines have a fishhook at the end and are most difficult to remove. You must have either a heavy glove or, best, a comb. Place the teeth of the comb among the spines near the skin and pull the cholla bud off. You will be surprised at how far out the skin comes before the spines pull loose.

*Maneating Limestone*

Another unlikely villain, this time mineral, is the "carnivorous" limestone. When limestone weathers in the rain a sinister two-dimensional sawblade effect is produced not unlike a rock's being covered with shark teeth. Throw your hand out onto this kind of rock and you will live to regret it.

*Healthy Canyon*

Except for the possibility of polluted water, the Canyon Backcountry is a healthy place – most cuts and scrapes heal without treatment. Unfortunately, the same cannot be said for a well-populated place like Phantom Ranch.

*ACCIDENTS*

Over the last 20 years my companions and I have accumulated over 2500 person days of off-trail hiking in the Grand Canyon backcountry. The mishap record of all that combined experience has been only two badly twisted ankles, one cut hand and two scorpion stings. I have already described my problems with scorpions, and the hand, cut by a sharp piece of schist, healed rapidly with the help of some butterfly stitches. The strained ankles were potentially more serious –

no ankle, no walk. It is interesting and instructive that both ankles were injured on the first day of a hike.

*Twisted Ankle* My treatment for a twisted ankle is this: make camp, leave the boot on, loosen the laces and take something for the pain. The next day you can lighten the victim's load and give him a walking stick if he doesn't already have one. When this happened to me, I moved slowly – but at least I could move.

Be aware, however, that my suggestion is counter to Red Cross First Aid protocol which recommends treating all ankle injuries as fractures. My treatment obviously does not allow walking. If you think your ankle might be broken then treat it as broken and stay off it.

*Emergency* I urge you to carry a signal mirror and know how to use it. In addition, you can use your sleeping bag and your ground cloth (folded into a strip) to put out international distress signals: "X" means "unable to proceed", "I" means "need a doctor", "F" means "need food and water." If you can get to the river, you will find boat parties anxious to help, if they can. If they can't, they can at least carry a message to the outside.

If you signal for help, put up a streamer that will tell the helicopter pilot about wind conditions and, if necessary, clear a flat place for him to land. Don't approach the helicopter until told to by the pilot.

*FOOD* Don't carry too much. It makes sense to carry extra food for emergencies, but don't overdo it. It doesn't make sense to carry out several pounds of it because you overestimated your needs. By the end of a trip I am sometimes made to feel like "a lion in a den of Daniels" – to use a quote from the famous New Mexico writer, Gene Rhodes – when over-supplied companions try to foist off extra food on me in the name of kindness.

How much food is needed? By food I mean all consumables except alcohol. The Institute for Health Maintenance, Albuquerque, NM, has a table of caloric requirements for various activities. Here are pertinent entries:

Resting: .5 cal/lb/hr = $12 \times W$ calories per day

Mountain Hiking: 1.0 cal/lb/hr = $H \times (W + P)$ calories per day

W = your weight in pounds

H = number of hours spent hiking (don't count rests)

P = weight of your pack in pounds.

For example, a 180 pound man with a 40 pound pack hiking for 6 hours a day needs roughly

$$12 \times 180 + 6 \times (180 + 40) = 3480 \text{ cal/day.}$$

Now we convert calories to food weight. The following table of calories per ounce for various camping foods is derived from *Nutritive Value of American Foods*, Agriculture Handbook #456, U.S. Department of Agriculture, 1975:

| | | | |
|---|---|---|---|
| water packed tuna | 40 | cereal, hard candy, cheddar cheese | 110 |
| oil packed tuna, cheese spread, dried fruits | 80 | granola bars, salami | 125 |
| | | peanuts, cashews | 165 |
| lentils, rice, spaghetti, ramen, dried non-fat milk, beans, gatorade | 100 | almonds, walnuts | 180 |
| | | pecans, liquid margarine | 200 |

Some fatty foods, like oil packed tuna and salami, are lower in calories than you expect because they still contain a lot of water. Correcting these calories for percent water gives 160 cal/oz for oil packed tuna and 185 cal/oz for salami.

*Use Sauces*

A French proverb says, "A sauce makes even fish taste good." So, too, a good sauce improves a mediocre camping cuisine. Cook bits of meat at home in teriyaki, sweet and sour or BBQ sauce and then dehydrate. After rehydrating add them and more of the same sauce to ramen.

*Quick Meal*

A good quick meal for two uses a 7.25 oz package of macaroni and cheese and small cans of tuna and chopped green chilis. The flavor contributed by the tuna and chili is well worth their weight, though I have taken to dehydrating the chilis.

*Look Ma, No Stove*

You can have good dinners without a stove by cooking, and dehydrating, them at home. Since the meal is ready to eat when it rehydrates, let it do so in a dark pot in the sun. You will have a warm meal, maybe even a hot one, without a stove.

*WATER*

I sweat a lot, and having run out of water twice, I am sensitive to the water problem. I believe if you don't have some left when you make camp you didn't start with enough. I seldom leave a water source without a half gallon in my pack and even then I would first inhaust almost to the point of gurgling when I walk. I like the word "inhaust." I found it in a Readers' Digest article on camels that inhaust 30 gallons at a whack. A kind of opposite to "exhaust."

*Water*  There are three reasons for taking a lot of water. One, you
*Needs*  dehydrate faster than you expect in the hot dry environment
of the Grand Canyon – remember Lake Mead loses 15 vertical
feet of water every year to evaporation. Two, anything you
eat, like lunch, requires water to process. Three, your water
needs increase substantially if you have any kind of accident.
Possibly, it may only slow you down or force you into a
bivouac but, at worst, it might force you into an evacuation
– all away from water.

*Use*  I recommend carrying your water in several small containers
*Small*  rather than in one or two large ones. If one cracks or ruptures
*Containers*  – in a fall, for example – you haven't lost as much. I use half
gallon plastic milk/juice containers and carry a spare cap. I
also carry a third cap which I have perforated for use as an
improvised shower head when sunwarmed water is available. If additional carrying capacity is needed, try putting a
Ziploc bag full of water in a pot.

*Drink*  And drink your water. This may sound strange, but people
*Your*  have died of dehydration with water in their packs. The fact
*Water*  is that dehydration often occurs faster than your efforts to
rehydrate can counter it. It takes time for swallowed water
to get to the tissues. Besides maintaining proper electrolyte
levels, use of an additive like Gatorade or ERG will also help
water be absorbed more quickly. Continual consumption of
water is important because a little dehydration causes a
substantial loss of physical function. Additives are useful,
too, as a consumption aid – the water tastes so good you
drink more.

*Drink*  The current formula for my very popular drink mix is:
*Mix*  Lemon/Lime Gatorade for 24 quarts — one package
Iced tea mix for 12 quarts — one cup
Lemon/Lime Crystalite for 16 quarts — eight cuplets
Tang for 6 quarts — one jar
Mix well and use one ounce in a quart of water.

*Heat*  Heat cramps are a symptom of electrolyte imbalance. When
*Cramps*  they occur, stop for a rest and drink some of your mix. If it
does not contain electrolytes then add a salt tablet to each
quart. Try to get the kind of salt tablet that contains potassium. In an emergency I have licked the sweat off my arms.
My rule is: if salt tastes good, I probably need some.

Water is purified in three ways. Ordered by effectiveness these are: boiling, filtering and the adding of chemicals. *Purify Water*

The Park Service still recommends boiling for at least ten minutes as the only sure way to purify water. However, recent medical studies indicate that Giardia cysts are killed at temperatures well below the boiling point of water – 140 to 150 degrees Fahrenheit for one minute. This means that just bringing water to a boil is more than sufficient to kill Giardia cysts. I have also found that boiling helps clear up dirty water by creating a scum which can be scraped off.

Filters are popular, and there are several on the market. I have used both the Katadyne and First Need and am reluctant to recommend either because they clog so easily in dirty pothole water; the Katadyne filter can be removed for cleaning, but in one case I was doing that every three strokes. The Katadyne weighs 24 ounces, and 24 ounces of fuel will boil alot of water. So my advice is this. If you're willing to carry the water you need and forgo the freedom of purifying a cup when you want one, then carry extra fuel and forget the filter.

My recipe, somewhat simplified, for chemical purification is: 25cc of a saturated water solution of iodine per half gallon of water. I use a little more if the water being purified is cold or cloudy. Let sit for at least 30 minutes, up to an hour if the water is cold. Overnight is best.

If you have a choice, explore for a new route FROM water and not TO water. For example, if you are searching for a route through the Redwall in Haunted Canyon start from the stream at the bottom. Do not come down from the rim and contour into Haunted Canyon looking for a way down. You may not find one before you run out of water. *Exploring*

Look for cans of beer and pop in eddies below a rapid. Look also where driftwood has collected at higher water. I have probably found 99 cans of beer and once a friend found a can of Tuborg Gold high up in a tamarisk. On my through-Canyon hike, we stumbled on a cache of 24 cases. A note attached to the cache said, "Hi, Steve, Ralph, Bill et al, this is for you." Since my brother, who was with us, is named Al, it was obvious we were included in the invitation. *Eddy Combing*

*How*   How much water is enough? It is useful to think of water
*Much*   consumption in the same terms as a car's gasoline consump-
*Water?*  tion; that is, in miles per gallon. An Air Force survival
manual I have says you will be lucky to get 10 miles per
gallon in a desert environment. I have used a quart per hour
when it was 110° F in the shade – about 4 miles per gallon –
but that's extreme. I think 10 miles per gallon is about right;
so for trips taken at sensible times, a gallon should get you
from one night's water to the next. A half gallon may do in
cool weather.

*Faint*  If you are following a faint trail and lose it, the chances are
*Trail*  it went up and you didn't. Look for it above you.

*Waistband*  I unfasten my waistband when I cross a deep or fast moving
stream – whether wading in the water or walking on a log –
I can shuck my pack more quickly if I fall in. I even follow
this rule when traversing a cliff above the river.

*The*  The game of "what if?" is a game all can play. Many things
*Game*  can go wrong during a hike and which of these many
*of*  mishaps you choose to protect yourself against depends on
*What If?*  your temperment. My wife, for example, considers mainly
medical problems, and once she was able to save a life by
producing epinepherine to treat anaphylaxis. I, on the other
hand, consider mainly mechanical problems, i.e., equipment
failures. Two of my "what ifs?" are the following.

I carry a spare set of shoulder straps attached to the large
stuff bag I have for my sleeping bag. Thus, the stuff bag
doubles as a day pack. I also take a spare clevis and spare
clevis pins and lock rings. The pins and lock rings are stored
in unused holes on my pack frame.

*Healthy*  Heat and moisture are hazardous to the health of my feet. I
*Feet*  take my boots off when I rest and let them and my feet and
socks dry. If the socks don't dry enough, I change them.

Although the trend is toward lighter boots for off-trail
hiking, I am old fashioned and prefer a leather boot with
good ankle support and a stitched sole. Two weak-ankled
companions, with many miles under their soles, use a light
boot with a thin, laced, inner canvas "sock" with steel ankle
supports. Still others, who carry superheavy packs, get by
somehow with only jogging shoes – sometimes with toes
worn and side seams split. Because ankles and, to a lesser
extent, knees are skeletal weakpoints, care must be taken to
protect them. So wear light boots if you must, but be

prepared to fall rather than put sudden awkward stresses on an ankle or knee.

Off trail hiking causes a different pattern of boot wear. Some good advice for preparing new leather boots for rough use was given to me by a backcountry ranger: fill the toe seam across the front of the boot with epoxy cement before you do anything else to them.

*Sunburn*

Sunburned skin doesn't sweat well. I use a long sleeved shirt and a long billed visor over a bandana on my balding head. I should use a sun screen. Long pants are useful for brush.

*Shelter*

An overhang is the most satisfying shelter for me, and during the years when rain seemed to be rarer than it is now, especially in the fall, it was sometimes the only shelter I had. More recently, with inceasing rainfall – both week-long trips in the fall of '87 had only one non-theatening day each – I have begun taking a 10'x10' tarp. Originally, I strung it up with a variety of long lines, but water tended to puddle and start leaks and in '87 I experimented with using the tarp in a sort of half cylinder. First, I rig a taut line between two walking sticks. Then I bend an eleven-foot lightweight folding aluminum tent pole and hold it in an arc with string. This arc is tied at right angles to the taut line and helps support it. The tarp is put over the whole thing.

The supporting arc creates the feeling of considerably more room than you would have with just a triangular cross section and stakes keep everything tight. The result is an effective free-standing tentlike structure, roomy for four and adequate for five if you scrunch together a little. My pack remains outside with a garbage bag over it. One night it drizzled for almost eight hours straight and the only water problem we had was due to inadequate trenching on the uphill side of the structure. The total weight for this shelter for five is two and a half pounds.

*Walking Stick*

I find a walking stick very helpful, especially when going down steep places. It is also useful as a third leg when crossing a swift stream like Tapeats Creek. A ski pole without the basket makes a good one.

*Choose Your Companions With Care*

Choose your companion(s) with care. This may sound like a strange comment, but the psychology of off-trail hiking in the Canyon is at least as important as the physiology. I remember one youngster who was so upset about not being on a trail that I built ducks as I went along to give him the illusion of a trail. The ducks were removed by a confederate hiking last. These hikes are not to be taken lightly. If you are the leader, think carefully about taking people you don't know.

There are at least three things to consider. First, is the potential companion physically capable of backcountry hiking? It is hard to imagine more difficult hiking anywhere in the United States and, in my opinion, the principal reason for this is the urgent need to reach water within a certain length of time. Sometimes, this requirement makes for long and very difficult days.

Second, many people who are capable of difficult Grand Canyon hiking just don't like the indefiniteness of cross country travel – they are never completely at ease with their surroundings. Usually they aren't as perceptive as a young companion who explained after a trip was over that he didn't feel comfortable during the hike until he had made the conscious decision to trust me – he had realized he no longer had control of his own destiny and that I, as leader, had it instead. Some strongminded independent people cannot give up that sense of control. They are difficult people to have along on a trip.

Third, avoid having a group whose members have widely disparate hiking and climbing skills unless the leader is prepared to travel only as fast as the slowest member. It may also be helpful to have companions who are capable in dealing with emergencies.

Something that happened to some friends – thank God it didn't happen to me – illustrates this perfectly. It was a hike off Atoka Point for members of the New Mexico Mountain Club and a long first day of sidehilling through heavy brush made it especially difficult. Once down by the River, one mountain climber type decided he had had enough and wanted up and out. He could not find the way he had come and other efforts to get out were thwarted by Redwall cliffs. He left the group and although his progress for the next days paralleled the group's, though sometimes heard, he was not seen. He reappeared when the group reached the rim. This is an extreme example, but it shows what can happen to someone hiking in the Grand Canyon whose behavior on other hikes and climbs seemed normal.

A friend of a friend can sometimes mean trouble. One seriously thought his friend was trying to kill him and his friendship with my friend ended as a result. Another was disturbed by a downclimb in a steep ravine, and I told him to take a cord and lower his pack; instead, he threw it off the cliff. It fell ten feet and rolled and bounced another fifteen. Fortunately, nothing was broken. I think he hoped something would break so he could go back.

I was talking to yet another "friend of a friend" after a long day on the "freefall" shortcut into Nankoweap and noticed his shoulders didn't look symmetrical. I asked about it and found he had a Harrington rod in his back. These rods are embedded under the skin along the spine to correct severe curvature of the spine by having the vertebra clamped to it. The top of the rod is anchored to the lower neck and the bottom to the pelvis. The wearer of such a rod cannot bend his back except at the waist. The man had two large raw ulcerated areas on his lower back where the rod anchors made bumps in the skin which rubbed on his pack. No wonder all he could think of when he got to the creek was how he was going to get out. Strangest of all was that this man's friend didn't know about the rod.

*NOTATION*

The word "River" refers to the Colorado River.

A duck is a small cairn of at least three rocks. Because two rocks can sometimes get piled on top of each other naturally there is the saying, "two rocks do not a duck make."

The word "Canyon" refers to the Grand Canyon.

I follow Harvey Butchart's device, used in his three *Treks* volumes, for locating myself on a map not only by terrain features but also by cartographic ones.

*BOOKS*

Butchart, Harvey   *Grand Canyon Treks*
                     *Grand Canyon Treks II* and *III*
                     La Siesta Press, 1970, 1975, 1984.
These books have information about hiking routes in Canyon backcountry that you won't find anywhere else. The author has made a special study of routes of historical interest.

Collier, Michael   *An Introduction to Grand Canyon Geology*
                     Grand Canyon Natural History Association, 1980.
I think this is a wonderful book. There are other geology books on the Canyon with more detail and bigger words, but I think Collier's book is the place to start. He gives a feeling for what is happening that I haven't found anywhere else.

Crumbo, Kim          *A River Runner's Guide to the History of*
                     *the Grand Canyon*
                     Johnson Books, 1981.
This book should appeal to hikers as well as river runners –
they both view the Canyon from the bottom. The author has
a readable style and Edward Abbey wrote a controversial
foreword.

Hamblin, W.K. &      *Guidebook to the Colorado River, Part 1:*
Rigby, J.K.          *Lee's Ferry to Phantom Ranch in Grand*
                     *Canyon National Park*
                     BYU, 1968.

                     *Guidebook to the Colorado River, Part 2:*
                     *Phantom Ranch in Grand Canyon National*
                     *Park to Lake Mead, Arizona-Nevada*
                     BYU, 1969.
These two books tell you in great detail what's happening,
geologically speaking, along the river. I like the set of aerial
photographs, and I like the diagrams showing the rise and
fall of the strata as you proceed downstream.

Redfern, Ron         *Corridors of Time*
                     Times Books, 1980.
I bought seven copies of this book when it came out – four
for myself and my children and three for my brother and
his. What clinched the sale were the pictures. He has pano-
ramic photographs that are almost better than the real thing.

Whitney, Stephen     *A Field Guide to the Grand Canyon*
                     William Morrow & Company, 1982.
This book tries to cover everything you may want to know
about the Canyon – animal, vegetable or mineral. For the
most part it succeeds. It is good for keying out plants and
animals. It is adequate on geology, but sketchy on insects.

Breed, W.J. &        *Geology of the Grand Canyon*
Roat, E., editors    Museum of Northern Arizona & Grand
                     Canyon Natural History Association,
                     Third Edition, 1978.
This is a collection of papers by experts in Grand Canyon
geology that is rewarding for the dedicated reader.

Wallace, Robert      *The Grand Canyon*
                     Time, Inc., 1973.
A good first book with which to get acquainted with the
Grand Canyon. It has an interesting and informative text
and fine pictures.

# — 2 —

# PHANTOM CREEK CRYSTAL CREEK LOOP

A general statement of condition:
*"Up schist creek."*
author unknown

| | |
|---|---|
| 6 days plus layover day(s), if any. | ***LENGTH*** |
| Dragon Spring on the first day and Upper Phantom Creek on the last. | ***WATER*** |
| Bright Angel, Arizona | ***QUAD*** |
| DeMotte Park, Arizona (used only for small part of access road) | ***MAPS (15')*** |
| On road to Tiyo Point | ***ROADHEAD*** |
| Turn west off the highway to the North Rim about one half mile north of the road to Point Imperial. A sign indicates that this side road takes you to the Widfors Point Trailhead. | ***ROUTE TO ROADHEAD*** |

After 0.9 miles you reach a locked gate. This gate appears after you pass the parking lot for the Widfors Point Trail and turn left at a "Y". Remember to get the current combination to the lock when you get your permit.

After 3.2 miles you enter a meadow and come to a fork – go left. The right fork leads to Point Sublime. A tiny sign a few inches off the ground points the way to Tiyo Point.

After about 4.8 miles you should park. Even allowing time to get the combination right, it takes only 40 minutes from the highway to your parking spot on the Tiyo Point road.

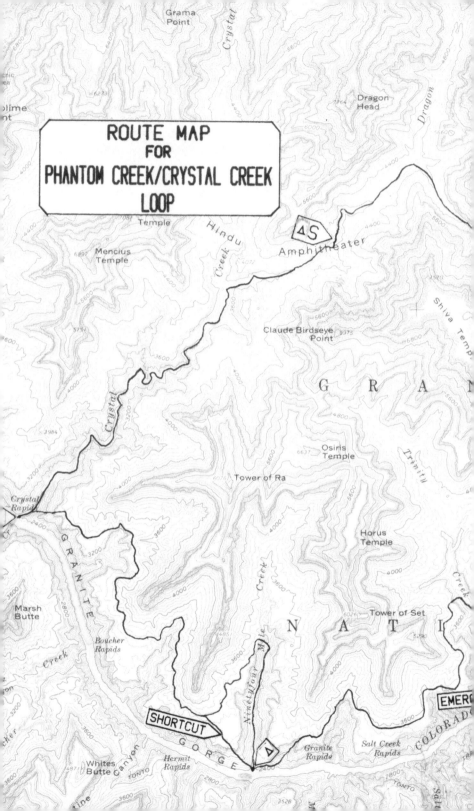

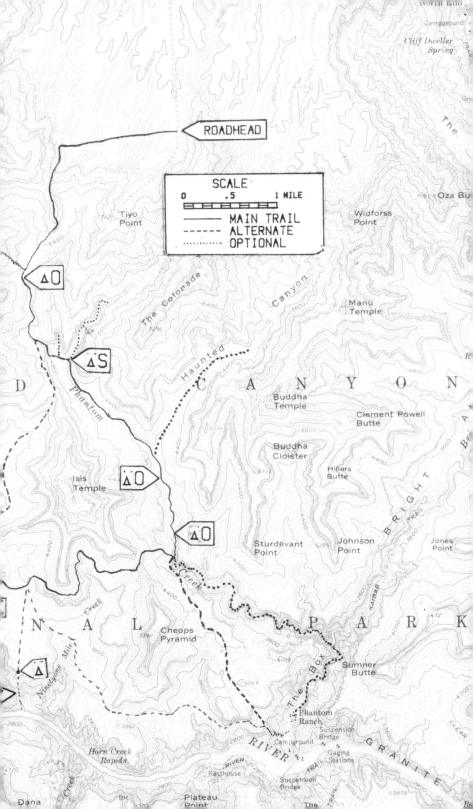

*HIKING*
*TIMES*

| | Use Areas | Locations | Elapsed Times Between Locations (hours) |
|---|---|---|---|
| Δ | Outlet | Car | |
| | | | 1:00 |
| | | Rim takeoff point | |
| | | | 2:00 |
| Δ | Phantom Creek/Trinity (dry camp) | Shiva Saddle | |
| | | | 4:00 |
| Δ | Trinity | Dragon Spring | |
| | | | 5:30 |
| Δ | Trinity | Mouth of Crystal Creek | |
| | | | 1:30 |
| | | Tonto above Crystal Creek | |
| | | | 6:15 |
| | | Top of 94 Mile descent | |
| | | | 1:30 |
| Δ | Trinity | Mouth of 94 Mile Creek | |
| | | | 1:30 |
| | | Tonto above 94 Mile Creek | |
| | | | 3:15 |
| Δ | Trinity (dry camp) | Bed of Trinity Creek | |
| | | | 3:15 |
| | | Cheops/Isis Saddle | |
| | | | 1:00 |
| Δ | Phantom Creek | 3600' contour | |
| | | | 2:30 |
| Δ | Phantom Creek | "Hippie" Camp | |
| | | | 2:30 |
| | | Top of Redwall climb | |
| | | | 2:45 |
| Δ | Phantom Creek/Trinity (dry camp) | Shiva Saddle | |
| | | | 2:00 |
| | | Rim | |
| | | | 1:00 |
| Δ | Outlet | Car | |

By 1987 I had done all the elements of this loop – and its alternates – separately except for the Redwall climbing route in Upper Phantom; so it seemed a natural trip on which to take my brother and some of his climbing buddies for their annual Canyon outing. We also had the opportunity to enjoy the company of one of the North Rim Backcountry rangers.

This hike was written up by Steve Roper for the November, 1988 issue of *Backpacker*.

*ROUTE*
*DETAILS*

The rim takeoff for this loop is off a point about .75 miles west-northwest of Tiyo Point. A V-shaped notch in the 7600-foot contour marks the descent ravine. To get to this notch I suggest parking about a quarter mile north of the bend in the road (about 1.3 miles north of the end of the road) and then heading west to the last ridge before the notch ravine. In getting there you will cross four other major ravines and, depending on where you have parked, possibly a fifth shallower one. You are on the right ridge when you can see canyon beyond the rim on the other side of the notch ravine. Head down this ridge to the rim and then descend westward into the notch ravine.

Another route to the notch point uses the spur road taking off near a point on the map by the first "T" in "Tiyo Point Trail" and heads down the ridge from the end of this road. It should work but I have not used it for two reasons: (i) I never thought of it and (ii) I would worry about finding my car on the return. If you park where I suggest, then on reaching the rim on the return all you do is head east to be assured of hitting the road – not necessarily hitting your car but at least hitting the road. Using Amundsen's idea for marking his food caches so he could find them on his return from the South Pole, you can mark the road every hundred yards each side of the car in such a way that when you find a mark it tells you which way to the car and how far.

*Rim*
*Takeoff*

Descend the notch ravine – there is a trail – and contour around to a ridge heading south. Follow this ridge to the end and look for a trail off the east side, close to the point. It takes you through the last Toroweap cliffs and then contours west a bit before descending through the Coconino and Hermit to the saddle northeast of Shiva Temple. This descent is tedious but straightforward.

*Shiva*
*Saddle*

Shiva Saddle is broad and dotted with big Supai boulders that can collect water during a rain; but don't count on finding any unless you are there within a few days of the rain. I have been told that there is a small spring in the Supai just below and to the west of the saddle on the north side. Look for some bright telltale greenery as a clue to its location before spending time searching for it. I looked for it once but couldn't find it. I suspect it is seasonal.

The route off the saddle is to the north where it is narrowest. After you get a little way down, the routes proliferate and you take your pick. Usually I end up taking one that veers off to the east to join the main drainage from the northeast via a fairly large tributary. Only minor obstacles remain before reaching the main Dragon drainage

*Dragon Spring* Dragon Spring is below an impassable chockstone near the start of the Tapeats narrows. On the Quad map it is about .15 miles north of a point between the "e" and "a" in "Hindu Amphitheater". Bypass the chockstone to the south by climbing out of the drainage at the "S" bend north of the last "t" in "Amphitheater" and going down a slope to a ravine that leads to the spring. You will hear the spring long before you see it. The spring has been running well the four times I have been there – once in July, once in September and twice in October.

It is an easy day from the Dragon Spring to the mouth of Crystal Creek. The water in Crystal Creek is almost too warm for swimming on hot summer afternoons but there is a big pool beneath a fifteen foot waterfall about a half hour from the mouth that feels somewhat cooler.

*Crystal Creek* If you keep left as you approach the vegetative tangle at the mouth of the creek, you will find a trail that takes you up to a bluff overlooking the rapids and then down to grassy banks by the River. While you're on the bluff, look along the skyline on the east side of the creek for a ramp leading through the Tapeats Sandstone to the Tonto Platform. This is your exit from Crystal. I usually get to the ramp by going up a ridge a little bit to the south and then contouring over to it.

The rapid at the mouth of Crystal Creek has been a major rapid only since the Great Flood of December, 1966. At certain water levels it is a fearsome rapid and several people have lost their lives in its wild water. Many of the commercial trips and all, I suspect, of the private ones stop at the upstream beach so the boatmen, I should say "boatpersons", can climb this bluff and see what they are up against. The severity of a rapid changes radically with river flow and it pays to check current conditions.

*The Great Flood of 1966* A word about the 1966 flood. An estimated 14 inches of rain fell in the area around the North Rim Entrance Station during 5-7 December, 1966. Although the area of maximum rainfall was quite small – an estimated 14 square miles – a great deal of this water found its way into Dragon Creek and its tributaries. Extensive measurements were made at a site about a half mile downstream from where the descent ravine from Shiva Saddle meets Dragon Creek. One estimate of the flow at this site was 29,000 cfs – I repeat, twenty nine thousand cfs. Nowadays, this is considered a high flow for the Colorado River.

The first and last phases of flow were mainly water but the middle phase, the maximum flow, was a mudflow. A mudflow is a mix of everything – rocks, trees, sand, water – and it is estimated that the mudflow was 18-20 feet deep in a 60 foot wide channel at the Dragon Creek site mentioned above. The way the mud stood up in blobs around the edges of the flow indicated it had the consistency of cake dough. The fact that 800 to 900 year old ruins were either washed away or buried indicates this mudflow was the highest in 800 to 900 years. Perhaps the most noticeable result of the flood was the transforming of Crystal Rapid from a pussycat to man-eating lion.

The details of the flood given above were taken from the pamphlet "Effects of the Catastrophic Flood of December 1966, North Rim Area, Eastern Grand Canyon, Arizona" by M.E. Cooley, B.N. Aldridge and R.C. Euler. It was published in 1977 by the U.S. Government Printing Office as Geological Survey Professional Paper 980.

*Route to 94 Mile*

Once on the Tonto our next goal was 94 Mile Creek, and all we had to do to get there was "contour around." I hate those words. They are a euphemism for big trouble. Contouring around sounds so easy, yet it is often so hard.

*Route Off Tonto*

There are two ways off the Tonto to the mouth of 94 Mile. One is a sporting descent through the Tapeats cliff due north of the "E" in "GORGE" and just west of the point. A good system of ledges takes you to a pair of chimneys. I had trouble finding the route down because we were approaching it for the first time from the Crystal side. My brother and I had ducked the route in 1982 but these ducks were almost invisible in 1987. The problem is that the route doesn't look possible from above because the final descent chimney can't be seen very well from there. On our descent in 1987 we put many ducks along the route so now it should be easier to find.

The top cairn is about 100 yards west of the point. Descend there to a broad ledge about eight feet down. Contour east to a chimney and descend about 25 feet to another ledge. Contour east again to another chimney and descend to the talus. Once there you have an easy scramble to the mouth of the creek. I don't hesitate to recommend this route. Good handholds and footholds abound and there is almost no feeling of exposure.

If this Tapeats route is not to your liking or you can't find it, you must contour into 94 Mile Creek and descend to the bed near the "i" in "Mile." Going down the bed of 94 Mile is easy. Salty water that gets saltier the farther south you find it often flows in the bed in the spring. I have found no water at all there in the fall.

*Route to Trinity Creek* The way back to the Tonto on the east side of 94 Mile is through the notch just west of the words "Granite Rapids." Once you get on the Tonto it is about three hours of "contouring around" to get to the bed of Trinity Creek. The descent into Trinity Creek is via the slope on the north side of the small drainage coming in west of the "k" in "Creek." Water collects in the bed of Trinity during a rain but the water I have found there is filled with bugs and suspended sediments. You need a filter system like First Need or Katadyn to make it potable. The next good water on this route is from Phantom Creek.

*Exit from Trinity Creek* The exit from Trinity is through a fault crossing the arm of Trinity heading northeast just south of the "k" in "Creek." This fault shows up as a transverse ravine cutting across the exit drainage near the 3520-foot contour. When you emerge from Trinity, head east up the talus to the top of the Quartzite cliffs. The geology of this region between Trinity and Phantom Creeks is a strong brew of the familiar and unfamiliar. Most of it is pretty much like it is everywhere else, but the rest is sometimes very confusing. For example, the Shinumo Quartzite is at least 250 million years older than the Tapeats Sandstone and thus should be lower, yet in this place it is higher. The Fault Map will show you what you are seeing and why.

*Route to Saddle* There is a fairly good deer trail on top of the Quartzite and you should try to find it. But watch it carefully as it circles the bay on the south side of Isis Temple. Before the trail crosses the drainage it goes down steeply. It is lost in the jumble at the bottom of the drainage and reappears on the top of the Quartzite on the other side. If the trail continues up to the Cheops/Isis saddle, I have not found it.

There is a good trail on the Phantom side of the saddle.

Follow it north for a few hundred yards until a spur trail takes off to the right and descends quickly in the direction of the red hillside (Hakatai Shale) across the way. Look for a thin broken up place in the cliffs in front of you where a ridge of talus comes up from Phantom Creek. The trail goes steeply down to the creek just upstream from the Narrows.

*Phantom Creek*

According to the Backcountry Management Plan, Phantom Creek is closed to camping below the 3600-foot contour. It would appear from the Fault Map that this contour is near the upstream limit of the red hillside of Hakatai Shale. Fortunately, this is where the big pools are.

*Layover Day*

If you allow a layover day at this beautiful place, you can have more than just the pools to occupy you. One thing to do is to make a quick trip to Phantom Ranch and back. At the beginning of the gorge there is a 20-foot waterfall. To get around it you can climb down a rope placed a few feet downstream from the fall on the west or you can go up on the east and contour around for a quarter mile or more to a ravine where you can get back down to the creek. Without a pack you need about three hours to go from the barrier fall to Phantom Ranch. Unless it is summer you will probably want to bypass the pools with vertical sides. One has a cable along a cliff to make it easier to get around it.

Exploring Haunted Canyon is something else to do on a layover day and so is exploring Outlet Canyon (the drainage north of the Colonade) or the Narrows at the head of Phantom Canyon, both up near the "Hippie Camp." There is no easy way out of Outlet Canyon, but in the Fall of 1975 a young man came over Shiva Saddle from Dragon Creek, took a wrong turn, ran out of water and tried to find an easy way in. He got part way through the Redwall someplace in Outlet by jumping. He reached water but he fractured his skull and broke his legs in the process – one had a compound fracture as I remember. His body was found several days later. This is what can easily happen if you forget the injunction always to explore *from* water and not *to* water.

*Hippie Camp*

It is about 2.5 hours from the 3600-foot contour camp to the Hippie Camp at the junction of Phantom Creek with Outlet Canyon – the drainage on the north side of The Colonade. The water in Phantom Creek comes and goes once you pass Haunted, but there is a small flow of water at this junction.

I call it the "Hippie Camp" because a colony of hippies

lived in Upper Phantom at one time and this camp has several constructions that indicate more than a casual occupancy. One is a good-sized stone bench – we used it as a kitchen table, another is a small path lined with river washed stones leading from the main living area to a lower terrace, and yet others are a small rock-lined nook and fire pit behind a large rock.

*Redwall* *Route* The route through the Redwall begins a quarter mile up Phantom Creek from the Hippie Camp, just past a drainage that goes west. There is a cairn marking where you leave the bed and head up a ridge. Most people, I think, don't go that far before climbing up through small Muav ledges to the same ridge. Eventually, ravines on each side of the ridge meet so that you cross a narrow isthmus to the base of the first of the two 40-foot climbs. My brother and a fellow climber went up without aid with their packs on, but I and a fellow non-climber needed a belay. This first climb is at enough of an angle to the vertical that hauling packs is awkward; so, somewhat reluctantly, we also climbed with our packs on.

The second 40-foot pitch is much like the first – just a bit steeper. Both have good rock and good holds. It took us an hour from the bed to the top of the first pitch and another half hour to the top of the second, which is at the same level as the horizontal traverse ledge. We negotiated this ledge without incident. When you enter the exit ravine at the end of the ledge be sure you go up the small gully that parallels the main ravine to the south. You can climb out of the main ravine, but there are some dry waterfalls to contend with.

All in all, this Redwall route was easier than I expected. Nowhere was there the gutwrenching feeling of exposure. Yes, I might have fallen 40 feet, but I certainly didn't have the feeling of falling more than that. There was always something fairly close below to stop you. Even on the traverse ledge, which – except in one place – was quite like a highway, I had no feeling of the possibility of a fall – the 400 feet to the bottom was not a concern.

*Route* *to* *Shiva* *Saddle* The basic instructions for the route from the top of the Redwall to Shiva Saddle are to go up if you can and to contour right if you can't. Looking north in the direction of the saddle (you can't see it) from the top of the Redwall, you get a foreshortened view of the Supai so that the middle cliffs form the skyline. The "basic instructions" take you north up the talus to the bottom of a set of three cliffs. You work your way up through the bottom two and then contour right to a point and then up through the last cliff to what was the skyline when viewed from below. The Fault Map shows a fault going through the narrow part of the saddle and since you can't climb through the remaining cliffs, you should contour right to this fault ravine. It is an easy scramble to Shiva Saddle. The elapsed time from the bottom of the Supai to the saddle was 2.5 hours.

We carried enough water to be able to camp on the saddle, but since we were there early enough we dumped most of the water out and continued on up to the car. If we had camped there we could have used a big overhang just east of the point where we gained the level of the saddle. It could sleep ten easily and had a large firepit carefully shielded from prying eyes on the South Rim.

The route back to your car from the saddle is the reverse of your route down except for the tricky part of reaching the road in the right place. I hate to say this, but we were off by 400 yards.

The Phantom Creek/Crystal Creek Loop can be started at Phantom Ranch. This option means the loop can be done by people travelling without a car and at times when the North Rim roads may be closed because of excess rain, fire hazard or snow. *ALTERNATE ROUTINGS*

There is also another option: you do not have to do the Redwall climb. All these options are described below.

There are at least two ways to Upper Phantom Creek from Phantom Ranch. I have already mentioned one: just go up the creek. This will be difficult during times of high water, but during normal times this is fairly easy even with heavy packs. There is, of course, the problem of the waterfall at the end, but if a trustworthy rope is there even that obstacle is fairly easy. If there is no rope, or if you don't trust the one that is there, then you must either make the climb – I have used a small crack at the lower end of the pool on the west side – or you must backtrack about 500 yards to a fault ravine on the east side. You will have to climb about five hundred feet before contouring around and down. I have never done this though I have seen it from the other side. Harvey Butchart mentions it, though, on page 68 of *Grand Canyon Treks III*. *Loop Begins at Phantom Ranch*

*Utah* Another route takes you onto the Tonto and across Utah
*Flats* Flats. This bit of Tonto has that name because it reminded
someone of the slickrock country of southern Utah. A faint
trail up through the schist begins at the northern end of the
northernmost campsite – just north of the bridge at the
upper end of Bright Angel Campground. It climbs steeply in
a northwesterly direction and eventually reaches the northern end of a long ridge which shows clearly in the 3200-foot
contour. A better trail takes you from there through the
Tapeats to Utah Flats. Cheops Pyramid is the predominant
terrain feature once you are on the "Flats", and you want to
head to the east of it.

If you make a detour to the east to look over the cliff,
don't be misled into thinking you want to be on the trail you
see hundreds of feet below you. Stay on the level you're on.

I found no trail through here but a good one appears as
you begin crossing the many drainages on the northeast side
of Cheops between the contour designation "4400" and the
word "Creek". Begin your descent to Phantom Creek via
faint switchbacks in the ravine just east of the southeast arm
of Isis Temple. Contour north around the shoulder and then
down to the creek – about at the 3600-foot contour, a few
hundred yards upstream from the waterfall at the end of the
gorge. You will find good shelter under big overhangs 15
minutes upstream on the east and 45 minutes upstream on
the west.

Because it is easier for a "non climber" to climb up than
down, both the basic routing and this alternative routing are
arranged so the Redwall climb is up instead of down.

*Low* Your return to Phantom Ranch from 94 Mile Creek need not
*Level* take you over the Cheops/Isis saddle. If you started from 94
*Route* Mile with enough water for a dry camp, or if you find
*to* suitable water in Trinity, you can take a Tonto-level route
*Phantom* instead. As you near Phantom Ranch, it is tempting to try
*Ranch* to contour around on the red rubble of the Hakatai Shale,
but this formation is unyielding and very difficult for the
edge of your boot to dig into. To avoid it, I climb up to the
base of the Quartzite cliff where there is about a foot of flat
ground and the going is much easier. You have to climb up
and later back down, but I think it is worth it.

When you reach the fault ravine heading up to the 4049-
foot benchmark on Utah Flats, you will notice that the
Supergroup has disappeared and the schist is in its familiar

place beneath the Tapeats. Cross the fault ravine, head for the long ridge on the rim of Bright Angel Creek due west of the word "Ranch" and find the rudimentary trail that takes you down to the campground. You will already have used this route if you have gone to Upper Phantom via Utah Flats.

If you don't have enough water for a dry camp enroute from 94 Mile to Bright Angel Creek and either need or wish to make one, let me suggest the Tapeats rim northeast of the "N" in "Ninetyone Mile Creek." I discovered a route to the river there under what I consider unusual circumstances.

I had planned a loop hike like the one I am describing, except it avoided the Redwall climb in Upper Phantom, and had looked at the copy of Harvey Jutchart's map in the Backcountry Office that showed all the places he had been. One of the lines on the map was off the tip of the plateau between Trinity and 91 Mile and down to the river – near the "3" in the contour designation "3600" – where I have suggested you camp. My plan was to use this route to go to the river and bring water back for a cache to be used on our return.

*Emergency Route to River*

I expected a "walkdown" kind of break in the Tapeats, but when I got there all I found were Tapeats cliffs everywhere. After considerable searching by all members of the party, I found myself sitting disconsolately on the edge of the Tonto wondering what to do next. Suddenly I realized that I was sitting right by the route.

The "route" turned out to be a four-foot crack straight down through the Tapeats to the schist below. The far side of the crack was some ten feet or so higher than the near side and there were many small ledges on both sides. By leaning across the four-foot width of the crack – with the schist clearly visible a hundred feet below – and using the small ledges alternately, it was possible to "ratchet" down to a broader ledge some eight to ten feet below and then walk along it to where the sides of the crack came together in a "V". The "V" was filled with rubble and slanted enough to make the rest of the descent fairly easy. Then it was an easy scramble to the bed of 91 Mile and down it a short distance to the river.

At the end of the trip I asked each of my companions – high school juniors – what they thought was the hardest part of the trip. And I asked them independently so one answer would not influence another. Unanimously and without hesitation they all had said, "Climbing down that crack and especially the leaning out across it to get started." One wiseguy added, "But I figured that if any old man could do it then I could. . .I mean .. .any 51 year old man."

The next time I saw the ranger who had showed me the Butchart map, I chided him about what was being offered as a "route." I felt it might be dangerous for some of the less experienced people who might use it. He said, "show me," and I looked again at the map. The route I had used was gone – it had been erased. I was the victim of a copying error. The original map is kept in a safe place and only a copy subjected to everyday use. Apparently, I had looked at a new copy that hadn't been checked against the original until after I had used it.

I offer this Tapeats route only as an emergency because, although it is safe enough, it will probably be frightening to some. Since it takes so much time to lower and, the next day, to raise packs, I suggest camping on the rim and making a water run to the River.

*Loop*     While it is easy to modify the basic loop to allow for starting
*Avoids*   it at Phantom Ranch, it is not so easy to modify it to eliminate
*Redwall*  the Redwall climb. The problem is water. If you do the climb,
*Climb*    there is no problem on either the first or last day because both first water and last water are close enough to the rim. Without the climb, however, one or the other of those days will be a rough one.

*Start*    First, let me suppose you are starting the loop at Tiyo Point.
*at*       The route to Phantom Creek is the same as described in the
*Tiyo*     basic routing, although I strongly recommend you cache at
*Point*    least a half gallon of water per person at Shiva Saddle.

The routing from Phantom Creek to Shiva Saddle is back over the Cheops/Isis saddle to the Trinity drainage and up the northeast arm of Trinity Creek to the saddle between Shiva Temple and Isis Temple. It is about an hour from this saddle to the top of the Redwall above the climb where the basic routing to Shiva Saddle takes over. I recommend starting from Phantom Creek with at least one and a half gallons of water. Hopefully, you will still have a half gallon left when you reach the Shiva Saddle. When this is combined with the half gallon you left there on the way down, there should be enough for dinner, breakfast the next morning and the hike back to the car.

If the loop begins at the Bright Angel Campground, the problem is the same but the solution is different. I suggest a dry camp at the head of the fault ravine into Trinity southwest of Isis Temple. From there it is a four-hour round trip to the River for water via the Emergency Route described earlier. Bring back enough so you have plenty for dinner and breakfast and can still cache a gallon per person for the return from Shiva Saddle. *Start at Bright Angel Campground*

Having that much water cached means you have a choice when you get to it on the way back; you can camp there and go over to Phantom Creek or around to the campground the next day, or you can continue on over to Phantom Creek the same day.

The route from the Campground to the dry camp at the top of the Trinity fault ravine is the reverse of one described above. Similarly, the routing from Trinity to 94 Mile Creek to Crystal Creek to Dragon Spring and thence to Shiva Saddle is the reverse of the one described at the beginning. The fault ravine on the south side of Shiva Saddle is still the best way for the descent and I don't think it matters how far down you go before contouring south as long as you get through the top Supai cliffs. When you get to the top of the Redwall continue south to the thin ridge just west of the "P" in "Phantom Creek."

The Redwall is broken up on the SW side of this ridge by a fault which, unfortunately, doesn't do the same on the other side and the descent to the Tonto is without incident. I have used the fault ravines to cross the drainage from the southwest side of Isis – one of these figured in the exit from Trinity on the way to the Cheops/Isis saddle in the basic routing – and you are now close to the water cache left earlier on your way to 94 Mile Creek. You can now retrace your steps to Bright Angel Creek or go over the Cheops/Isis saddle to Upper Phantom Creek.

*HIKING TIMES FOR ALTERNATE ROUTINGS* The following tables of hiking times show how the basic routing is modified to avoid the Redwall climb.

| Locations | Elapsed Times Between Locations (hours) |
|---|---|
| **LOOP BEGINS AT PHANTOM RANCH** | |
| TO UPPER PHANTOM CREEK VIA CREEK | |
| Bright Angel Campground | |
| | 5:00 |
| Phantom Creek (3600' contour) | |
| TO UPPER PHANTOM CREEK VIA UTAH FLATS | |
| Bright Angel Campground | |
| | 2:00 |
| Top of Tapeats (Utah Flats) | |
| | 2:30 |
| Phantom Creek (3600' contour) | |
| **LOOP AVOIDS REDWALL CLIMB** | |
| LOOP BEGINS AT BRIGHT ANGEL CAMPGROUND | |
| Bright Angel Campground | |
| | 4:30 |
| Top of Fault Ravine into Trinity | |
| | 5:45 |
| 94 Mile Creek | |
| | 7:30 |
| Mouth of Crystal Creek | |
| | 9:30 |
| Shiva Saddle (dry camp) | |
| | 5:45 |
| Water Cache | |
| | 3:15 |
| Phantom Creek (3600' contour) | |
| | 5:00 |
| Bright Angel Campground | |
| LOOP BEGINS AT TIYO POINT | |
| Car | |
| | 3:00 |
| Shiva Saddle | |
| | 4:00 |
| Dragon Spring | |
| | 5:30 |
| Mouth of Crystal Creek | |
| | 9:15 |
| 94 Mile Creek | |
| | 9:00 |
| Phantom Creek (3600' contour) | |
| | 9:30 |
| Shiva Saddle (dry camp) | |
| | 3:00 |
| Car | |

# — 3 —

# TUNA CREEK SHINUMO CREEK LOOP

On the value of a small libation (margarita) before fixing dinner:
*"It dulls the sharp edge of pain."*

Al Steck

| | |
|---|---|
| 7 days plus layover day(s), if any. | *LENGTH* |
| First water on way down is in Tapeats; next is at river. No water on Tonto traverses except in potholes after a rain. Last water on way out is in lower Flint drainage. | *WATER* |
| Bright Angel, Arizona<br>De Motte Park, Arizona<br>Havasupai Point, Arizona<br>Powell Plateau, Arizona | *QUAD MAPS (15')* |
| The roadhead is along the road to Point Sublime, about a half mile north of the sharp turn by the narrow neck on the way to the point. Park just up the road (north) from the beginnings of a drainage on the west side of the road. | *ROADHEAD* |
| There are two routes to the roadhead. Neither is routinely maintained and I sometimes find an axe and large pruning saw to be necessary. One route is via the road that also goes to Tiyo Point. Turn off the highway to the North Rim about one-half mile north of the road to Point Imperial. A sign at this side road points the way to the Widfors Point Trail. | *ROUTES TO ROADHEAD* |

*From* After 0.9 miles you reach a gate. This happens after you
*the* have left the highway, gone past the parking lot for the
*East* Widfors Point Trail and turned left at a "Y". The gate has a
combination lock and you should get the combination when
you get your permit.

After 3.2 miles you enter a meadow and come to a fork;
go right. The road to the left goes to Tiyo Point (a very small
sign a few inches off the ground points left and says "Tiyo
Point").

After 7.5 miles over a very bad road you meet the other
road to Point Sublime. At this intersection there is a sign
pointing back the way you've come saying "Tiyo Point".

After 5.6 miles you reach the Point Sublime campsites.

This route is not suitable for passenger cars. My VW bus
made it – but barely.

*From* The other route to Point Sublime starts outside the Park
*the* where Highway US 67 passes Deer Lake, just south of Kaibab
*West* Lodge and 26.7 miles south of Jacob Lake. Turn west on
Forest Service Road (FS) 422.

After 2.1 miles, at the top of the hill, turn sharply left onto
FS 270.

After .8 miles FS 222 goes to the right; you go straight.

After 1.3 miles turn right onto FS 223.

After 2.4 miles you meet FS 223A; go straight.

After 3.5 miles turn left onto FS 268.

After 1.1 miles veer left onto FS 268B.

After .5 miles you cross the Park boundary.

After .3 miles you meet the road to Swamp Point; go left.

After 1.0 miles you pass a faint road (with sign) to Tipover
Spring; go straight.

After 2.0 miles there is a road to the right; go straight.

After 2.4 miles a road merges from the left; go straight.
This is the Old Point Sublime Road that goes back to the
highway near the Entrance Station. This road should not be
used. There is a sign here that I find confusing when I am
going the other way. Make a note to go left at this sign on
the return.

After .1 miles there is a road off to the right that goes to a
cabin; go straight.

After .2 miles go sharply right and down one side of a
triangular intersection.

After 2.6 miles you reach the Tiyo Point Road junction
mentioned above; go straight.

After 5.6 miles you reach Point Sublime.

It is 25.9 miles from the Deer Lake turnoff to Point Sublime by this route. I don't think a passenger car can make it, but my VW bus did.

| Use Areas | Locations | Elapsed Times Between Locations (hours) | HIKING TIMES |
|---|---|---|---|
| ⊿ Point Sublime | Car | | |
| | Rim | :45 | |
| ⊿ Scorpion Ridge (dry camp) | Flint/Tuna Saddle | 1:45 | |
| ⊿ Scorpion Ridge | Tapeats Spring | 3:15 | |
| ⊿ Scorpion Ridge | River at Nixon Rock | 3:00 | |
| | Tapeats Rim | 1:30 | |
| | Monadnock descent canyon | 3:00 | |
| ⊿ Scorpion Ridge | Monadnock Amphitheater camp | 2:00 | |
| | Tapeats rim overlooking Hotauta | 4:45 | |
| ⊿ North Bass | Beach upstream Shinumo Rapids | 1:30 | |
| | Shinumo Creek via high trail | :45 | |
| ⊿ North Bass | Bass Camp Historical Site | :15 | |
| ⊿ North Bass | White Creek | 1:00 | |
| ⊿ Scorpion Ridge | Flint/Shinumo confluence | 1:45 | |
| | Base of Redwall | 2:00 | |
| | Top of Redwall | 2:15 | |
| ⊿ Scorpion Ridge (dry camp) | Flint/Tuna Saddle | 1:45 | |
| | Rim | 2:30 | |
| ⊿ Point Sublime | Car | 1:00 | |

By camping one night at the mouth of Hotauta Canyon (Scorpion Ridge Use Area) and the next at the Flint/Shinumo confluence, you can avoid camping in the North Bass Use Area. This will be necessary when, as it often is, the North Bass Use Area is full.

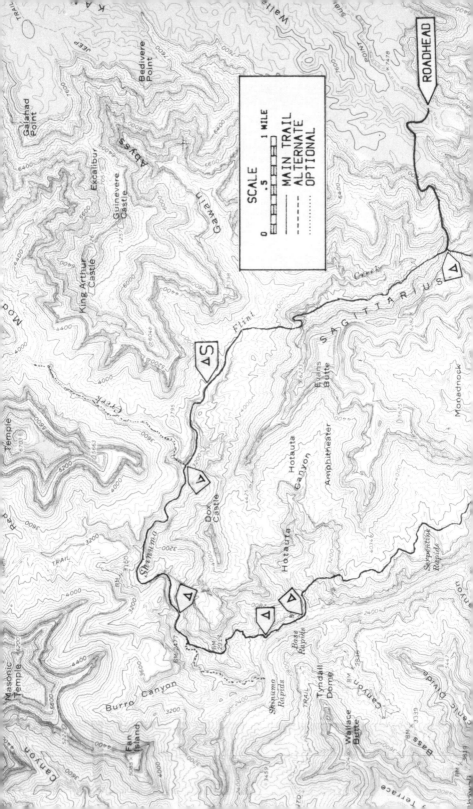

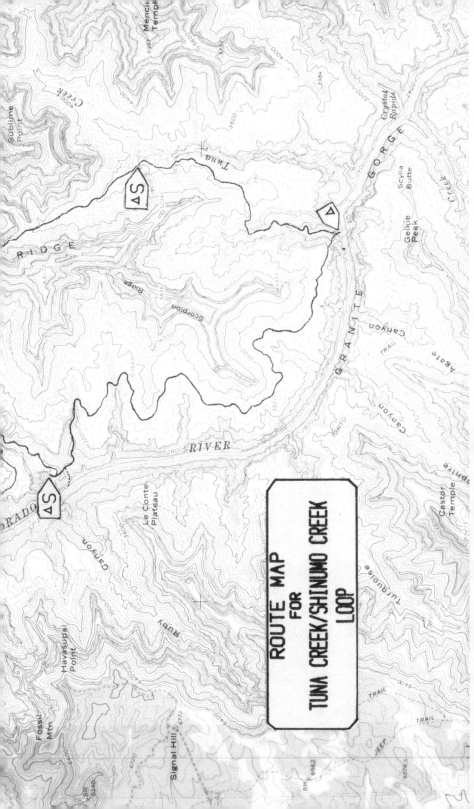

ROUTE MAP
FOR
TUNA CREEK/SHINUMO CREEK
LOOP

*ROUTE*  Where you camp the first night depends on when you leave
*DETAILS*  the car. The hiking time to the River for me is just under nine
hours, so you may not get there in one day unless you
camped the previous night at Point Sublime. Good camping
spots for the first night are the Flint/Tuna Saddle (dry camp)
and the Tapeats Spring.

After leaving the car and climbing the ridge, keep going
west until it begins sloping west into the next drainage.
Head north along the ridge until you reach a north facing
slope and can descend to the drainage. This gets you to the
bottom without any cliffs but you will be cursing the thorns
of the New Mexico Locust. I wear gloves and long pants.
After reaching the bottom, go down a few hundred yards
until you find a convenient place to climb out. Head west
again to a point at the rim between the "2" and the "0" in
the contour designation "7200". Search along the rim until
you have a steep talus slope in front of you that lines up
with a drainage heading all the way down through the Supai.

*Rim*  The rim takeoff is down this very steep limestone talus.
*Takeoff*  Eventually you must go south around the small red promontory below you, but there are many small cliffs in between.
No lowering of packs should be necessary. A good rule to
follow is: if you are in a good place to climb down one of
these cliffs, do so; if not, contour left until you can. I find it
helpful to leave small ducks for myself for the return trip. If
you do, be sure to remove them on the way out.

As you round the promontory you will find there is still
one last Toroweap cliff below you. Contour south on the top
of this cliff – I found a small trail (deer?) – until you can get
through it to the top of the Coconino, only moderately steep
here. I prefer to contour around a little farther and go through
the cliff to a ridge which shows clearly on the map as a
ripple in the contours immediately north of the Flint drainage
marked in blue that flows west toward the Flint/Tuna saddle
before heading north.

This ridge takes you through the Coconino and the Hermit
Shale and ends in the Flint drainage near the top of the
Supai. Continue down the bed into the Supai until you can
contour over to the Flint/Tuna saddle. The saddle is only a
quarter mile or so away, but the way is slow – brushy and
sidehill steep – and it seems much farther.

Try to leave the rim with enough water so that at least a
quart per person can be left at the saddle to be picked up on

the return. Some V-8 juice (for electrolytes) and/or a can of fruit (for carbohydrates) will also be appreciated then, too. I suggest beginning the loop down the Tuna drainage because it leaves the best part of the trip for last.

The Flint/Tuna saddle is about half way through the Supai so that not much Supai remains in the descent to the top of the Redwall. The route is south down the talus, but be careful of large (half-ton) rocks that are precariously balanced. A large recent rockfall covers a good deal of the slope – at least it seemed new in 1985 and I don't remember seeing it in 1977.

*Flint/Tuna Saddle*

Soon after entering the Redwall there is a dropoff that is bypassed up and over a shoulder to the east. If you go down the shoulder, be careful of the "carnivorous" limestone. It is helpful to wear gloves.

Once you are back in the bed there are only two more dropoffs of any consequence and both have obvious bypasses to the west. One might even have a pothole of water right at the lip. I have never drunk from it but I have used the water to cool myself off a bit. I have always bypassed the second dropoff by contouring a few hundred yards over to a break in a small cliff above a long talus slope. But in 1984 my brother found a deer trail that led over the rim of the dropoff to a small ledge that takes you to the main bed more directly. His way is a definite improvement over mine.

*Redwall Dropoffs*

Below this last dropoff the way is clear to the top of the Tapeats. Someone has been down Tuna through the schist to the River but I'm not sure how easy it was. In any case, there has been a small flow of water in the bed at the top of the Tapeats, just above the confluence with the east arm of Tuna, each of the three times I have been there – once in July and twice in October. There is a more substantial flow – complete with polywogs, frogs, small skippers and the black larvae that you often find in side canyon fast water – just below the Tapeats/Schist contact. This small stream in the schist probably flows year round in a normal year.

*Tapeats Spring*

I have no love for these wiggly black Buffalo Gnat larvae, and once in trying to send a batch of them to their heavenly reward I found when I tried to dislodge them they still remained attached to the rock by a thin thread of something like spider silk and were able to climb back up it to their original position.

*Route to Tuna*  There is no particular reason to go to the mouth of Tuna, but if you do, my best route is to contour around on the west rim of Tuna to the notch at the point. A deer trail takes you from there to the bed of Tuna a few hundred yards inside the mouth. It is a hard two hours from the mouth of Tuna upstream to Crystal along the schist because it involves so much climbing up in and around the obstacles. It is also a difficult hour from Tuna down to the next drainage. The low level route runs into cliffs just upstream from that drainage and you have to wade about 20 feet to a sandbar along a narrow ledge about two feet under water or climb along the face of the cliff. I don't remember whether or not there is a way around above the cliff. Try to be here by 0900 for early morning low water or else the ledge may be too far under water.

*Tapeats Spring to River*  The easiest way to the drainage below Tuna is to cut over the saddle north of the small hill (height 3921 feet) just west of the Tuna drainage. A well-defined gully leads from the saddle to the Tapeats rim in front of you and for a while it looks like it will take you through the Tapeats. It won't, but just a few hundred feet farther north along the rim, near the "3" in "3200", there is an easy way through to the bed.

As you go down the bed, look closely at the Tapeats rim to the west for the climbing route out of the bed. It is a crack behind a pillar near the point at the mouth of the canyon. Only one bypass (to the west) is needed before you get to the River. There wasn't much beach in 1982 and after the flood of '83 there was even less. A big block in the middle of the River, which is very narrow here, creates a small rapid which provides a steady roar through the night. On page 78 of *The Colorado River in Grand Canyon – A Guide*, Larry Stevens calls this block, "Nixon Rock" – named by boatmen in honor of Nixon's departure from office.

*Climbing Route Out*  There are two ways back up to the Tonto. One is a direct climbing route, although you can keep your packs on. The other is more leisurely: just go back up the drainage for about a half-mile before turning to climb out. Both routes require starting back up the drainage except instead of returning to the bed at the bypass the direct route keeps on climbing. If you forgot to look for it coming down, just aim for a buttress that looks like it might be a tower with a chimney behind it.

This is a good route – direct, exciting and safe. There is good footing on a series of ledges, and getting up six feet to the first ledge is about the hardest part of the whole climb – especially now that I broke off one of the footholds. Follow these ledges until you can get under a chockstone that is wedged in near the top of the tower. Go under it, turn back to face it, and continue climbing up the ledges to the top.

You probably won't have noticed any exposure until you get on the other side of the chockstone and some may find a belay comforting at this point. Transferring yourself from the top of the tower to the mainland is somewhat unnerving, and eight different people on my last trip did this in eight different ways. The concensus was that the farther right you go the easier it is. Even with rests we took only an hour and a half from River to Tonto rim. We built a medium-sized cairn so others could find the route down from the top.

Once on the Tonto you contour around to the drainage just south of the one that drains the Monadnock Amphitheater; the one you want reaches the River about 0.4 miles upstream from the mouth of Ruby Canyon. If you can't get to the bed of this canyon easily, contour along the rim until you can. Go down it to the Tapeats pouroff and at the lip follow a ledge off to the left until you can get back to the bed. It was on this ledge that a high level Park Service official (who shall remain nameless) was crawling on his hands and knees under an overhang when his super-heavy pack shifted over his head and forced his nose into sudden and forceful contact with the Tapeats Sandstone. It was an industrial-strength nosebleed. *Route into Monadnock*

After negotiating a few obstacles in the bed of this drainage, you should begin looking for the place where you leave it. Look for a shoulder of schist ahead of you on the right with a white band of quartz leading up to it. When you can, leave the bed and climb up to this shoulder. It is about 0.2 miles northwest of the "3" in "3200", and you should aim for the 2880 foot contour. As you round this shoulder, contour over to a saddle to the northwest. From here you can look down to the bed of the Monadnock Amphitheater drainage. In October, 1982 there was a nice flow of water visible from the saddle, but in October, 1985 there was none. We did find a small flow a hundred yards or so down in the schist, but if you are at the saddle and don't see any water in the Monadnock drainage, you may wish to go down the broad slope to the southwest and get water at the Colorado River.

*Route*     I have not found any direct route out of the Monadnock
*Out of*    drainage to the north. Although we explored all the likely
*Monadnock* spots, we couldn't get out until a small ridge led up to some
Tapeats ledges just north of the "A" in "Amphitheater"
almost two miles up from the mouth. There are small seeps
and springs in the bed for about half that distance. Once on
the Tonto you continue contouring – for a while there is a
good deer trail – to the point looking down on the Hotauta
drainage. This is a great view and it is a good place for lunch.
Imagine, too, what Grand Canyon hiking would be like now
if Frank Brown had had his way and built a railroad through
the canyon. Down below you, in the flats east of the river,
there would now be a switching yard – Stanton named it
Dutton's Depot Grounds.

*The*     The story of Brown and Stanton and the plans for the railroad
*Brown*   has at least as much drama, adventure and irony as the
*Stanton* Powell one and should be more widely known. Once you
*Story*   get used to the idea that the immensity of the canyon does
not confer a corresponding immensity to the task – Stanton
argued that only the last 200 feet of depth made any differ-
ence – you can see that a railroad at the bottom of the Grand
Canyon is all too feasible. This is the story.

Railroads were big business in 1869 when the transconti-
nental railroad was completed. After Powell finished his trip
through the Grand Canyon in that same year, it was inevi-
table that someone would think of the canyon as a railroad
right of way. But, curiously, the person whose idea for a
canyon railroad finally produced results had never heard of
Powell's exploits.

All that S. S. Harper, prospector, cowboy and wanderer of
the Southwest, knew of railroads he gleaned from watching
a survey being run through the mountains of Arizona and
New Mexico. Yet, later, spending a day and a half at a place
historians think was Lee's Ferry, the advantages of a river
route to the sea occurred to him – no mountains, no snow,
level all the way. Harper must have thought the bottom of
the Grand Canyon was everywhere more or less the way it
was at Lee's Ferry.

Next comes Frank Mason Brown. I don't know how old
he was in 1889, but I would guess about forty. Old enough
to be an ex-California State Senator and to have made good
money in Denver real estate, yet young enough to be looking
for adventure and exciting investments. By all accounts he

was very personable, honest, frank, energetic, courageous and, above all, of a sanguine disposition.

In January of 1889 Harper went to Brown with a mining venture. Brown was not interested and said he'd rather invest in a railroad. You can guess the rest – Brown was off and running. In the next two months he got committments of $50,000,000 for a canyon railroad contingent on a favorable engineer's report.

On March 25th the Denver, Colorado Canyon and Pacific Railroad Company was formed with Brown as President. On March 26th an engineer was hired to run the survey down the Colorado River from Grand Junction to its confluence with the Green River. It began on March 28th. A main survey party would later continue the line to the Gulf of California. In April, Robert Brewster Stanton was hired to be chief engineer. Stanton's application is dated April 15th.

I give all these dates only to show Brown's energy and driving purpose – no flies could land on him.

*Stanton and the Georgetown Loop*

One of Stanton's early exploits is now a tourist attraction. In 1884, as a Division Engineer for Union Pacific, he built the Georgetown Loop. The Colorado towns of Georgetown and Silver Plume, now two miles apart on Interstate 70, near Loveland Pass and not too far west of Denver, had too steep a gradient between them for a railroad until Stanton designed a series of loops that stretched two miles into four and a half. This more than halved the gradient so a railroad could serve the mines at the upper town. Today, during the tourist season, a narrow gauge steam locomotive plies its way back and forth between Georgetown and Silver Plume so tourists can ride the loops and appreciate first hand Stanton's skill as an engineer. There was a two hour wait when I tried to ride it so I put off the experience to a later time.

If the Brown/Stanton story has a hero it is Stanton. He was a capable engineer and a good leader. It is too bad he wasn't on the scene in time to help with the planning. Brown consulted with Powell but apparently didn't listen when Powell described the dangers and impracticability of the venture. Powell's reservations were discounted because he wasn't an engineer. Stanton was later very bitter and criticized Powell for not making Brown aware of the hazards, but I believe that Powell was honest about them and that Brown erred in not hearing what he didn't wish to hear. Besides, I believe Powell wanted to discourage Brown. He saw the Grand Canyon in terms of water storage for the benefit of the arid west and Brown's railroad there did not fit his vision.

Brown's facility for selective hearing shows in his reaction to what Powell wrote him in reply to a request for advice about boats. Powell described his in detail, but the only message Brown seemed to get was that they were too heavy to portage easily. Consequently, Brown's boats were light – only 15 feet long, 40 inches wide and 18 inches deep. They were clinker built of thin, brittle red cedar planking with a round coppered bottom and weighed 150 pounds; Brown was being sure he could portage his boats easily.

*No Life Jackets* But having poor boats was not the main problem. There was also inadequate protection for food and for life itself. That's right, no life jackets. I'm not sure why. Some sources say he "forgot" them. But most say that, in spite of pleading to the contrary, he refused to take them on the grounds that they were an unnecessary encumbrance. But Brown was the boss, so no life jackets. Stanton, like Powell, had only one useful arm and he was urged to take one for himself, but he refused that advantage over his associates.

The Brown party left Green River, Utah, on May 25, 1889, exactly 20 years and a day from the time Powell had left Green River, Wyoming. The party had 16 people in six boats. Included in the group were two lawyers, friends of Brown from Denver, taken along as guests – were they investors or were they potential investors?

Getting the survey to the head of Cataract Canyon was easy, but getting through it was not. They soon lost one boat and more than half their food. Not far from the end of Cataract Canyon the lack of food produced a near mutiny and they split up. Brown and ten others took three boats and hurried to Dandy Crossing (Hite) for supplies while Stanton and the rest stayed behind to continue the survey. After several days of starvation rations, Stanton's group was resupplied from below.

Five people were left at Hite to run the survey through Glen Canyon to Lee's Ferry. Three, including one of the "guests", had had enough and went home. The other eight, including Stanton and Brown, plus an experienced boatman who joined them at Hite, hurried on to continue the survey from Lee's Ferry – where the other "guest" left. The Glen Canyon survey party was to have been resupplied from Lee's

Ferry but was not and abandoned its task.

So, on July 9th, eight people with no life jackets left Lee's *Brown*
Ferry in three frail boats. The next morning Brown's boat *Drowns*
capsized at an "eddy fence" at the foot of Soap Creek Rapid
and Brown was caught in the whirling eddy and drowned.
On July 15th two others were drowned in a rapid near Mile
25. One of these men was Peter Hansbrough. Later in the
year his body was found on a pile of driftwood near a place
now called "Point Hansbrough".

At this point Stanton wrote ". . . Two more faithful and
good men gone! Astonished and crushed by their loss, our
force too small to portage our boats, and our outfit and boats
unfit for such work, I decided to abandon the trip..." They
climbed out South Canyon after caching their gear in what
is now called "Stanton's Cave." They saw Brown's body go
by but could not retrieve it.

Stanton was back in Denver on July 27th. The company
was reorganized and Stanton put in charge of completing
the survey. Profiting from experience, he ordered better
boats, this time of oak, 22 feet long, 52 inches wide and 22
inches deep. He also ordered the best cork life preservers for
the passengers and watertight rubber bags for the food.

On December 10th (still 1889) the second party – 12 people
in three boats – left from a point near Hite to complete the
survey through Glen Canyon and on December 28th reen-
tered Marble Canyon. Four days later, on January 1st, the
photographer, Nims, fell while taking a picture and broke
his leg. He was evacuated to Lee's Ferry via Rider Canyon.

On February 6th, one boat was smashed into "toothpicks"
while shooting it unmanned through a rapid (à la Powell)
after portaging its contents. A few days later, at Crystal
Creek, the recruit from Hite left the party and made his way
to the rim and through the snow to Kanab. His route to the
rim is still a mystery. Because of the added weight of new
supplies taken on at Diamond Creek, the three men whose
boat had been lost above Crystal Creek were asked to leave
the group. On March 17th the party, now numbering seven,
reached Grand Wash Cliffs and on April 26th reached the
Gulf.

Stanton's survey through the Grand Canyon was not a *Survey*
detailed one. To save time and money – he was largely *Records*
financing it himself – he ran what he called an "instrumental

reconnaisance." This meant detailed notes on grade and canyon composition but with a detailed survey of only the hard stretches. There was also a detailed photographic record, including about 150 stereoptican views, so that skeptics could be convinced that written claims of feasibility were indeed true.

When Stanton took over the photographic duties after the evacuation of Nims, he did so with some trepidation because he had no knowledge of photography whatsoever. All that anyone knew was that you left the cap off a little longer when it was dark. Through both luck and foresight all the film from both expeditions survived without damage. On the second trip, the film was always stored in tins that were soldered shut. Over 2000 pictures were taken and no picture was lost except from inexperience and this loss was only about ten percent. From the historical point of view, these pictures are probably the most important result of the survey. We can be thankful it wasn't the railroad.

*Route* Two hundred yards or so east of the Hotauta overlook there
*off* is a break in the Tapeats which shows up nicely on the Fault
*Tonto* Map. Go down this break and contour northeast beneath a wall to a broad slope which leads to the bed of Hotauta Canyon. A nice bench by the River has a trail of sorts that leads to the large sandbar just upstream from Shinumo Creek.

*Shinumo* There are three ways to get to Shinumo Creek: (1) you can
*Creek* take a climbing route – which will be awkward with packs – over to the mouth of the creek; (2) you can take the trail shown on the map which perhaps takes you higher than necessary; or (3) you can take a lower trail that goes over a small saddle much closer to the River – about at the 2560- foot contour.

If, later, you follow the creek through the schist narrows to the River you will find only one obstacle: a chockstone above a magnificent pool. There are three ways around this chockstone: (1) climb down a hole nearby that leads to a grotto beneath it, or (2) bypass it on ledges and chimneys on the downstream side, or (3) jump off it into the pool.

*Bass* The Bass Camp Historical Site is an interesting place for a
*Camp* camp. It is only a short distance upstream from where the upper trail joins the creek. Across the creek from this junction, beyond the arrowweed flats near a big catclaw, you may be able to spot where Bass' trail takes off for his asbestos mines in Hakatai Canyon.

William Wallace Bass is an important figure in the history of the Grand Canyon of a hundred years ago. He set up camp near what is now the trailhead of the South Bass Trail in 1884 and lived there or at Bass Camp along Shinumo Creek for almost 40 years. He constructed what are now known as the North and South Bass trails for use by his dudes so he could take them across the Canyon. For a while he took them across the River by boat, but eventually he put in a cable which wasn't cut until 1968.

Bass also developed copper and asbestos mines and got a particularly good long staple asbestos from a mine in Hakatai Canyon. The fibers that are still seen littering the ground at the Shinumo Camp are up to two inches long and I remember reading somewhere that the mine produced ones that were even four inches long. Some of these fibers found their way into European theater curtains. *Asbestos Mine*

Across the creek from his camp, where the artifacts now are, is a broad flat alluvial plain where Bass had his orchard and garden. Nothing remains now except remnants of some irrigation ditches and a storage pond. If you follow the main ditch upstream along the cliff you will see where he drew his water from the creek. There is an iron rod on top of a small buttress at the creek's edge with wire trailing from it that I take to be a support for a flume that dipped into the creek near here. *Orchard*

A flat rock about a yard square and about two feet high between Bass Camp and the creek has a hole in it that mystifies me. I used to speculate that Bass had a small suspension bridge across the creek or a water wheel to assist in irrigation, but if that were the case there should be other holes on other rocks. There are likely candidates but no holes.

If you stay on the Bass Camp side of the creek enroute to the Flint/Shinumo confluence, you will nearly get cliffed out by the Shinumo Quartzite. You can get by, though, and just beyond where the sand broadens out again there are a variety of Indian ruins along the cliff – some granaries and a shelter. You will already have passed the "eye" granary but I'll leave that for you to find.

About an hour beyond the granaries you pass White Creek, which is the easiest way to Muav Saddle. I used the lower part of the North Bass Trail precisely once. The next dozen *White Creek* times I have used White Creek because it is so much easier and so much more pleasant.

*Flint* Going on up Shinumo Creek beyond White Creek is a
*Shinumo* struggle. It isn't really very difficult, but it is a struggle,
*Confluence* though nice pools make pleasant swimming in hot weather. It is about two hours from White Creek to the Flint/Shinumo junction and on the west wall above it there is an Indian ruin. A quarter mile or so down the creek from this junction on the south side I saw a nautiloid fossil on a faint trail where I was walking.

*Layover* A layover day spent in upper Shinumo is a day well spent.
*Day* If you continue on up the creek, you will get "pooled out".
*in Upper* There is a large over-your-head circular pool about a hundred
*Shinumo* yards from the Flint junction. It is great for swimming but a bit cold unless you are there at midday. To get past it, you must climb the schist at the mouth of Flint and pick up a trail near the bottom of the Tapeats. It will contour around and down to the creek several hundred yards above the pool. There are lots of cottonwoods and other pleasing greenery in happy contrast to the mainly thorny stuff elsewhere.

Without packs, you should, in a day's time, be able to get at least as far as the Merlin/Modred junction. There are some large and inviting pools where the Tapeats comes out so be sure to go at least that far.

*Rainbow* Both arms of Shinumo are fun to explore. My wife saw a
*Plateau* good-sized waterfall in the Modred arm. About an hour
*Loop* beyond the Modred junction, the creek turns sharply east and in another hour turns north again. This fault ravine leads to the rim if you are of an adventurous frame of mind. Together with the North Bass Trail, this route makes a nice loop that takes you around Rainbow Plateau. It will be described in another book.

*Wasps* It was in these parts that I once saw ten rattlesnakes in one week's time, never to see any there again. Another time I was sitting by a big cottonwood near the creek and heard a great whooping and yelling punctuated by a loud splash – more yelling and another splash – and then laughter. Four younger members of the party had disturbed some ground wasps which had chased the wildly vocalizing youngsters until they had jumped into a pool big enough to hide almost every square inch of all four of them until it was safe to emerge. I, too, was attacked by a swarm when I stepped on a rock that slid out from under me. I was stung fourteen times. This was in August. Other times of year have not produced such annoyances.

My usual equanimity was sorely tested here at the Flint/ *Tarantula*
Shinumo junction one summer night years ago. I always tell people with whom I'm camping in the Grand Canyon never to swat something crawling on you without first looking to see what it is. You certainly don't want to swat a scorpion. So the injunction is "brush – don't swat." That's fine in theory, but can you imagine the frustration of wanting to brush something off and not knowing exactly where or how hard to brush? The night in question was so warm that I was sleeping in my bathing suit on top of my sleeping bag. I was also lying on my back.

I awoke instantly with the first touch and could feel a tug at my skin as a foot tried to get a purchase on it. Something was lifting itself off the ground to begin climbing up onto my leg. Successive steps were slow and deliberate – like tiptoeing. What could it be? The night before, a frog had jumped onto my face and almost startled me into the next world. But a frog arrives suddenly and sits on you like a wet lump until, just as suddenly, it is gone. This was no frog. They don't tiptoe along your leg. Neither do chipmunks or squirrels.

What else could it be? I could feel each foot as it was carefully placed and couldn't help noticing the feet were very widely spaced. Whatever the "something" was, it was about the size of my hand. I wasn't about to swat but neither was I sure where to brush – that would obviously depend on how big the thing was. It slowly crossed my trunks and began its methodical way up my bare stomach. By this time I had a pretty good idea how many legs it had – certainly more than four. I was also sure that nothing this big would have only six. I didn't have to open my eyes to be sure it had eight – I knew it had eight.

But that was both good news and bad news. The good news was that I couldn't imagine a scorpion that big. If the thing working its way across my chest toward my neck were a scorpion it would have to be as big as a small lobster. The bad news was that if it weren't a scorpion it had to be a tarantula – and a big one at that. But the good part of the bad news was that tarantulas are not supposed to be very poisonous.

It was now stepping up off my chest and onto my chin and brushing it off was out of the question. I didn't want to make it angry. All I wanted was to appear absolutely and totally inedible. I wondered if it could sense my muscular tension and increasing pulse rate which, unfortunately, would signal just the opposite. The spider stepped on my lips, paused briefly at my nose – I was holding my breath – and stepped on an eyelid. I had been unable to open my eyes earlier and now it was obviously too late. I was still holding my breath as the tarantula proceeded slowly across my forehead, into my hair, back down to the ground and into the night.

*Up* Now it is time to talk about "up and out." It is a long way
*and* to the car from the Flint/Shinumo confluence and my "Hiking
*Out* Times" estimate 9½ hours; so if the days are short you may wish to camp on the saddle – not a bad idea in any case. If you do, you will be glad you left water for yourself.

*Redwall* Go up Flint about to the "F" in "Flint". This will take an
*Routes* hour. There is sometimes enough water to make it possible to camp up Flint a ways if you are in a hurry or if it is hot and you need an early start. The Redwall route is in a bay about a quarter mile northeast of the first "S" in "SAGITTARIUS". It is tempting to try to continue up Flint to the saddle, and I have done so, but getting out involves so much brush and complicated bypasses, that I think the way I will describe is easier. After you leave the Flint drainage, climb up along a ridge and through some small Muav cliffs to the base of the Redwall. The upper wall meets the lower at the far right hand side of the bay, where a scary 30-foot climb takes you to the bottom of the bay. There is a slightly less scary 20-foot climb on the far left hand side of the bay.

The rest is easy. Contour around and up to the base of a chimney high up on the far left hand side of the bay. After you climb it, you will be on a sharp ridge leading to the mainland. It is so sharp and so steep on each side that I prefer to be on all fours for the worst parts.

*Back* It is about two hours from the top of the Redwall to the
*in the* saddle, and my recommendation is not to climb the Supai
*Saddle* cliffs until you are almost under the saddle.

The first time I went up to the rim from the saddle, I went up the gully under the cliff that is to the south of the ridge I like to go down. Somewhere in there, below the Coconino, was a large Coconino boulder with a dinosaur track on it. I didn't see it and the person who did could not give an accurate description of where it was. So lots of luck if you look for it.

I will leave you on the saddle to retrace your steps to the car. As I said before, there will be less routefinding if you left small cairns for yourself on the way down. If you did, don't forget to remove them as you climb back out.

# — 4 —

# SHINUMO CREEK
# TAPEATS CREEK
# LOOP

## Circumambulation of Powell Plateau

A futile effort to explain why off-trail hiking on the Tonto is easy:
*"All you have to do is contour around."*

Don Mattox

9 days plus layover day(s), if any.            LENGTH

There may be stagnant pools at the top of the Redwall in    WATER
Saddle Canyon and often some flow in the middle of the
Redwall but don't count on it. Except for June 1988, there
has always been a good flow of water at the Saddle/Stina
junction. Occasional water surfaces in the bed between this
junction and the stream from Tapeats Cave and there is
usually water flowing out of Crazy Jug. There is no water
between Tapeats Creek and Stone Creek. You will have
frequent access to the River between Stone and Blacktail
Canyons and may even find some flow in the side canyons.
Blacktail has a small flow at or just inside the mouth. There
is access to the River at Explorers Monument between the
"L" and the second "O" in "COLORADO" on the topo map,
and there is a good flow in the drainage opposite a point
between the "G" and "R" in "GRANITE".

  Hakatai Canyon has water near the entry point, and Burro
Canyon has a modest seep in the bed where the trail crosses
it. Shinumo Creek and lower White Creek have plenty of
water. You will find good springs in the Tapeats Narrows
near the top of the Tapeats, in the bed near where the trail

starts up the Redwall and near the top of the Supai. Finally, a reliable spring is located at the base of the Coconino, at the southern end of the trail that contours into Muav Saddle from the south; it has served both horse and man for a long time.

QUAD         Powell Plateau, Arizona
MAPS (15')   Havasupai Point, Arizona
             Supai, Arizona (extreme upper right corner only)
             Kanab Point, Arizona (extreme lower right corner only)
             Taking a portion of the Park map is more useful and less expensive than taking the four individual quad maps. But remember that the cartographic descriptions may be different.

ROADHEAD     Swamp Point

ROUTE        Go south from Jacob Lake 26.7 miles (just down the hill past
TO           Deer Lake) and turn right on Forest Service Road (FS) 422.
ROADHEAD     After 2.1 miles, at the top of the hill, turn sharply left onto FS 270.
             After 0.8 miles FS 222 goes off to the right – go straight.
             After 1.3 miles turn right onto FS 223.
             After 2.4 miles you pass FS 223A – go straight.
             After 3.5 miles turn left onto FS 268.
             After 1.1 miles veer left onto FS 268B.
             After 0.5 miles you cross the Park boundary.
             After 0.3 miles you reach a delta intersection. Turn right on the road to Swamp Point.
             After 7.6 miles you reach the end of the road at Swamp Point. These last seven and a half miles are difficult for a passenger car but it can be done. It is easy going with a VW Bus.

| HIKING TIMES | | Elapsed Times Between Locations | |
| --- | --- | --- | --- |
| Use Areas | Locations | 1981 | 1988 |
| Δ Swamp Ridge | Swamp Point (car) | | |
| | | :30 | :45 |
| Δ Powell Plateau | Muav Saddle | | |
| | | 5:00 | 8:00 |
| Δ Blacktail | Stina/Saddle Canyon Junction | | |
| | | 2:00 | 3:15 |
| Δ Tapeats Amph. | Junction with Tapeats Cave Canyon | | |

| | | | |
|---|---|---|---|
| Δ Tapeats Amph. | Junction with Tapeats Cave Canyon | | |
| Δ Tapeats/Upper | Thunder River | 2:30 | 2:30 |
| (Designated Site Camping only) | | | |
| | | 2:00 | 2:00 |
| | Point above mouth of Tapeats Creek | | |
| | | 2:30 | 2:30 |
| Δ Blacktail | Stone Creek | | |
| | | 1:15 | 1:30 |
| | Bedrock Canyon | | |
| | | 2:15 | 5:00 |
| Δ Blacktail | 128 Mile Canyon | | |
| | | 2:30 | 2:45 |
| | 127 Mile Canyon | | |
| | | 2:00 | 4:00 |
| Δ Blacktail | Fossil Rapids | | |
| | | 2:30 | 3:30 |
| Δ Blacktail | Forster Rapids | | |
| | | 2:00 | 2:45 |
| Δ Blacktail | Mouth of Blacktail Canyon | | |
| | | 3:15 | 4:15 |
| | Explorers Monument opposite Elves Chasm | | |
| | | 2:30 | 3:45 |
| Δ Blacktail | Good water opposite "R" in "GRANITE" | | |
| | | 4:00 | 5:00 |
| | Bed of Waltenburg Canyon | | |
| | | 2:15 | 3:15 |
| Δ Blacktail | Bed of Hakatai Canyon | | |
| | | 4:15 | 5:00 |
| Δ North Bass | Bass Camp Historical Site | | |
| | | 1:00 | 1:15 |
| Δ North Bass | White Creek/ Shinumo Creek Junction | | |
| | | 1:30 | 1:45 |
| Δ North Bass | Tapeats Chockstone and Spring | | |
| | | 2:00 | 3:15 |
| Δ North Bass | Bottom of Redwall | | |
| | | 2:00 | 2:15 |
| | Top of Redwall (bed of Muav Canyon) | | |
| | | 1:45 | 2:15 |
| Δ Powell Plateau | Muav Saddle | | |
| | | :45 | 1:15 |
| Δ Swamp Ridge | Swamp Point (car) | | |

* The 1988 times are longer because the author was seven years older (age 63) and because daytime temperatures were up to 114°F in the shade.

ROUTE MAP
FOR
SHINUMO CREEK/TAPEATS CREEK
LOOP

SCALE
0    .5    1 MILE
MAIN TRAIL
ALTERNATE
OPTIONAL

EMERGENCY

*ROUTE*  Powell Plateau is a large wooded island separated from the
*DETAILS*  Kaibab Plateau mainland of the North Rim by Muav Saddle.
It thrusts southwest from the saddle some six miles, causing
the Colorado River to make a detour and take twenty miles
to do what it could otherwise have done in ten. Unfortunately, fire destroyed some 3000 acres of Powell Plateau
during the summer of 1988.

The hike around Powell Plateau from car back to car –
about 50 miles – is the quintessential loop hike and the Muav
Fault, which joins the Shinumo and Tapeats drainages, makes
it possible.

*The*  The Muav Fault was not exploited as a highway right-of-way
*Muav*  as was the Bright Angel Fault, which provides the routing
*Fault*  for the Bright Angel and North Kaibab Trails, but the Muav
Canyon branch of the fault was used commercially by W. W.
Bass to bring his dudes up to the north rim. His route exists
today as the North Bass Trail. Don Mattox and I found out
in the late 60s that the Saddle Canyon branch was also
passable. Later we found Bass' old trail over to his asbestos
mine in Hakatai Canyon and made our way over into
Waltenburg Canyon. By this time I had also been from
Tapeats Creek over to Stone Creek, but in spite of all this
exploration I was surprised when in 1980 my friend Don
Mattox suggested we try a hike around Powell Plateau. This
was an inspired idea.

*First*  Even though I wasn't sure I was up to such an expedition,
*Try*  Don and I started down the North Bass Trail in early October
*1980*  1980. It was his first trip of the year and in spite of his
strength and endurance, he was woefully out of shape.
Usually I like hiking with Don because I figure that if I get
into trouble he can carry me out on top of his pack. He is
also the only person I know who puts his 60 + -pound pack
on by first laying it on the ground, reaching down with his
arms crossed and grabbing and swinging the pack over his
head so it slides down his arms and lands snugly on his
back.

But this time Don was having a bad time of it and was
really beat by the time we reached the White/Shinumo
confluence. The wine and fondue dinner revived both of us
somewhat. I learned, though, that the wee beasties that roam
at night do not eat fondue. They may eat my pack and my
bootlaces but they don't eat my fondue. Maybe real mice
don't eat quiche, either.

It took a while the next day to rediscover the route to Hakatai. *Route* Standing dripping with sweat on the lip of our descent route *to* into Hakatai and looking down the shimmering expanse of *Hakatai* Tonto between us and Explorers Monument, I had a strong *Canyon* "what am I doing here" feeling. Study from the south side of the River had led us to believe we might find a way down to it from Explorers Monument, but we couldn't be sure. Besides, that looked days away and we wished we knew how many hours it was to the next water after Hakatai. All we knew for sure was that there was none in Waltenburg.

It was our second day so we had many pounds of food and, *First* at eight pounds per gallon, the water was a burden, too. I *Try* was discouraged and ready to turn back. But it was Don's *a* trip and I couldn't very well ask him to go back. So I used *Failure* psychology. "Don", I said, "don't feel you have to make this trip on my account. It sure looks hot out there and I just enjoy being in the Canyon. I don't have to go around Powell Plateau." I made my plea short so the impact would be more subtle and we rested and downed a little more of my Gatorade/iced tea/Tang drink mix.

After a few minutes of enjoying the view of the sweltering chasm, I set the hook that I had so carefully presented. "Besides", I said, "I think we can do something else that hasn't been done before." I didn't know whether I was right or not, but it sounded good at the time. "A few years ago I found a Redwall route out of a branch of upper Merlin. We could use that, and as Harvey says, ' . . . there are many ways through the Supai . . . ' We could get back to the rim to the north, go across to the Swamp Point road and hike back to the car. If we can't go around Powell Plateau, we can at least go around Rainbow Plateau."

Don didn't say a thing. He just got up, slung on his pack and started back toward Shinumo Creek.

This ended our first try at going around Powell Plateau. We decided to be cleverer next time and start from the Tapeats side at a cooler time of year. That way we would be along water much longer at the beginning and would be in better shape and have lighter packs when we reached the waterless(?) stretch that defeated us the first time.

Now, a year later, in the middle of October 1981, Mattox *Second* and I and a young friend and fellow Grand Canyon explorer, *Try* Robert Benson Eschka (aka Robert Benson) were once again *1981* at Swamp Point ready to start down – this time down Saddle

Canyon. I had been down Saddle several times since first going down it with Don in 1969, and I was taking a tape recorder so I could make notes while I was hiking instead of while I was resting. This first try at high tech note-taking was not too successful. I got "on" and "off" mixed up so it was off when I was talking and on when I wasn't. I ended up with no data at all – just long stretches of heavy breathing, snatches of comments yelled back and forth and the incessant "click . . . click . . . click . . . " of my walking stick. It was just as well. I found I couldn't hike and dictate at the same time – like the man who couldn't walk and chew gum at the same time.

*Route* The route is straight down the drainage through the brush
*Down* to the big dropoff in the Supai. It was here years ago that
*Saddle* one of the youngsters in our party decided he had carried
*Canyon* his watermelon far enough. We all had a most refreshing break and he hid the rind behind a rock to be carried out on our return. At that time, a week later, we found all traces of rind had disappeared, eaten, I guess, by mice who found in those scraps an abundant supply of an otherwise rare commodity – water.

At this Supai dryfall we contoured left and up to a ridge, then down it a bit until we could descend westward to a minor drainage that quickly joined the main one. The ridge is just west of the "C" in "Saddle Canyon." Once back in the main drainage, we were at the top of the Redwall, and after a hundred yards or so, the bed – actually the line of the Muav Fault – being blocked by an ancient rock fall, turned sharply into a deep cleft which is wonderfully cool in summer.

*Redwall* We travelled down this drainage to the big fall at the Redwall pouroff near the junction with Stina. Although, in 1981, we found no serious obstacles in between, we were forced to lower packs at a few places. In 1988, we found one of these obstacles was more serious than it had been before. This obstacle is a chockstone that comes just after a 10-foot fall that can be downclimbed fairly easily. We didn't consider this chockstone a problem in 1981 because the bed was probably only five or six feet below it, but in 1988 with more efficient scouring, the bed was more like ten feet below it and we had to improvise something to lower ourselves. There is a bypass high on the right along the steeply sloping wall that I usually use going up Saddle Canyon; this time it seemed awkward for going down.

The first time we went down Saddle Canyon several of the obstacles seemed just bad enough that one of us jumped or climbed down each one and then climbed back up just to make sure we could get back up if the way was blocked below – thus avoiding the predicament that Abbey describes in *Desert Solitaire* when he jumps into a pool and just barely gets back up when further descent is impossible.

One obstacle provides a welcome diversion. It is the "Slicky Slide", a long 45-degree chute of polished limestone, sometimes with the added lubrication of water, algae and slimy moss. It is difficult to get down with a pack on your back because everything is so slippery. Two other possibilities are to lower the packs or wear them in front. And I forgot to mention that the slide ends in a frigid chocolaty pool which is of indeterminant depth until the first to descend checks it out.

*Slicky Slide*

If the packs are lowered and carried through the pool by one kind soul then the rest can bypass it dryshod by very careful cliff hanging. I call this route "Dale's High Water Low Level Traverse" in honor of its discoverer who was just an ordinary joe who didn't want to get his feet wet. I am amazed at how strong that motivation can sometimes be.

The final big drop into Stina at the Redwall pouroff comes fifteen minutes after the Slicky Slide and is bypassed along a narrow, steeply sloping bench leading to a talus slope. Once, our descent of this precarious tumble was greatly complicated by the angry attention of a swarm of wasps intent on stinging us to death. I have often camped at Stina and, except for 1988, there has been plenty of water and good camping on smooth level friendly Muav ledges.

*Good Camping at Stina*

But we didn't make camp here in 1981 and instead hurried on down the drainage in search of shelter from an impending storm. Just past Crazy Jug we found a good overhang with a level place just big enough for three as soon as we removed the small rock in the middle. It didn't take me long to find out that the "small" rock had humungous roots. I was ready to give up and move on when Mattox said he'd show us the Old Egyptian Rock Trick and get rid of it. He said the pyramids were built from the top down with each course of rocks being slid under the ones already in place after they had been raised using the OERT. There is no point in arguing with Mattox when he is like this. Just go along with what he says.

*The Old Egyptian Rock Trick* I completed the excavations to show our enemy in its true dimensions: roughly pyramidal, two feet high and one square foot in cross section at the base. At least 150 pounds to be lifted almost two feet. The OERT is best done with three people. Two can do it but it is much more work. One person sits on each side of the rock facing it and the third fills up the hole when you don't need it anymore. The first sitter-downer puts his feet against the rock and pushes as hard as he can so the top moves away from him slightly causing a small gap to appear under his side of the rock. The third person packs this gap with dirt. Then the second sitter-downer does the same thing on his side and the third person packs the new gap. When the first sitter-downer's second turn comes, everything is the same as before except the rock is perhaps a quarter inch higher.

At the end, instead of a small rock in the middle of a level floor, you have a big one – the hole having disappeared. But now it is easy to roll the rock off to one side. Our shelter was ready just about the time it began to drizzle.

*The Great Horned Snake* Since we are near Crazy Jug, I will tell another story. Crazy Jug is a pleasant canyon with small waterfalls, pools, narrows and friendly Muav ledges. It was up this canyon I once rescued a Great Horned Snake from starvation. Seeing it from a distance, I could see it was a monster – five feet of regular snake with three or four inch horns on each side of its head. I had visions of TV appearances – Johnny and David here I come – as the discoverer of a new species of snake, a Loch Ness creature of the Grand Canyon. But then the bubble burst and I saw that the "horns" were not horns at all. The snake had swallowed a bat without first gathering in the wings; the bat body was out of sight but the folded wings protruded symmetrically and looked like horns. It wasn't easy to remove the bat. Although the snake cooperated, the deed was difficult because snake teeth are all aligned the wrong way – down the throat to facilitate swallowing and to prevent the escape of prey. Soon my good deed was done and I anthropomorphized by wondering if there was a flicker of gratitude in that tiny brain. It was lucky it was not a rattlesnake. I think then I might not have risked the rescue.

*Tapeats Creek* Water came and went the next day as we proceeded down the canyon. For a while a substantial flow came above ground among cottonwoods near a fifteen-foot waterfall. But the main flow in Tapeats Creek doesn't come down Tapeats Creek; it comes down the canyon from Tapeats Cave. That's not to say flash floods don't come down Tapeats Creek. They do and I've seen one, but the source of all the creek water is near the cave.

Travel was not as easy when we reached the stream. There is enough water and a steep enough gradient that you don't cross with impunity. Sometimes, in late spring and early summer I don't dare cross it – period. A hundred yards or so of narrows is another place to be cautious. In the fall you can wade the narrows, and we did – except for Benson, who preferred to pioneer a high-level traverse of the cliffs on the west side. It took him quite a while but it is nice to know such a bypass exists.

*Designated Camp Sites*

The first of two sets of Tapeats Creek Designated Camp Sites is just below the junction of Tapeats Creek and Thunder River. The second set is on the beach at the mouth of the creek. The thousands of rafters who visit Thunder River every summer have turned a good trail from the River into a highway. But now in the fall there were very few boat visitors. The only people we saw were Park Service workers trying to reduce "multiple trailing" by planting chollas to block unwanted pathways. It seems to work.

About the same time a year later in about the same place, I ran into another NPS crew milling around in the brush with clipboards and when I asked one young lady what was going on, she said, "it's a sociological experiment to see how long it takes before one ranger flips out and kills another in the course of such tedious work." They were running a transect and counting all plants and plant types a half meter on each side of their line.

*Scorpion Terrace*

We wanted to get over to Stone Creek for camp so we didn't dawdle much on the way down. Except for lunch at Scorpion Terrace, where there is sort of a mini Niagara – a trio of falls in a "U" pouring into a narrow slot forming a cauldron of foaming white water. I call it "Scorpion Terrace" because it was there on one stormy night, complete with flash flood, that a friend was stung by a scorpion and had a very bad time of it – we had to shake her to get her to breathe.

*Jumping Fish Falls*

While resting there, Mattox said he saw a huge fish trying to jump the falls. This is a typical Mattox trick – a subtle form of oneupmanship – so we humored him by saying "yeah", "wow", "how big was it?" until finally there really was a big fish trying to jump the falls – two feet long, at least. After much more fish watching than we had time for, we were rewarded by seeing the "try, try again" philosophy eventually succeed.

From this fall it is only two creek crossings – or none if you contour around instead of crossing – to the place where the Stone Creek trail leaves Tapeats Creek and follows an emerging shelf of Bass Limestone. At this same place, the trail to the mouth of Tapeats Creek goes up the corresponding shelf on the other side of the creek.

*Stone Creek Trail* Upstream from the point above the Tapeats delta, the trail to Stone Creek comes and goes, but following the bench is easy. There are at least two ways off the nose at Stone Creek, but they are more easily found from below. We eventually gave up trying to find one from above and followed the now distinct trail around into and down Stone Creek. The sun had gone from the falls so we took only the briefest of showers before going down to camp by the Colorado River.

From now on – except for the quarter mile to the mouth of Galloway – it would be new territory for all of us. That is always exciting. We didn't expect to be turned back by anything insurmountable, but the unknown always adds a special flavor to an activity. I wondered, though, about how difficult it was going to be. Don didn't seem to care much one way or the other – he just takes what comes – and Robert, I expect, was hoping for "almost" impossible barriers to overcome. He liked his physical medicine strong.

*Route to Bedrock Canyon* It was easy going along the River for the first hour or so although it would certainly be more difficult when the water is higher. Getting to Bedrock Canyon is a process of avoiding being cliffed out by following a rising diabase sill, then climbing down to the River through some rather crumbly stuff (Hotauta Conglomerate?) and then taking another ramp into Bedrock. We crossed the canyon at the mouth, entering a little upcanyon on the north side and leaving by climbing the nose on the south side to the same ramp we entered on. The water in Bedrock didn't taste very good and we went to the River to pick up extra in case we had to make a dry camp farther on. The next drainage, about a half mile farther, had a fine flow of good water with dunking pools, so we had lunch there. I call this canyon "Switch Level Canyon" because we entered it on the Bass and left it on the Tonto.

So far we had stayed below the Tapeats, but now we had to climb up on top of it. We found a burro trail that made it easy to contour around the gullies and into 128 Mile Canyon – our goal for the day. The way into 128 Mile is via the first side canyon on the north about a half mile in from the point. It is opposite a steep exit chute. The top half of the descent is over talus and there is one pouroff that looks formidable until you get to the edge and can look over. Benson hiked down to the River to look for good campsites but there were none – not even on the delta. We ended up camping where we had entered the canyon. It was a fine place – a good flow of tasty water and an easy route back up to the Tonto.

*128 Mile Canyon*

The following year I was making the same trip in the reverse direction as part of a lengthwise traverse of the Grand Canyon, and found an easy way off the upstream nose to the mouth of 128 Mile where a deep, warm, grungy pool was backed up behind the sandbar at the mouth.

The next morning around 0830 we climbed back up onto the Tonto and followed the slowly-descending Tapeats. We had lunch, still on the Tonto, just downstream from Fossil Canyon. A little farther on, the Tonto disappears and we could hike along the River. An obnoxious travertine obstacle gave us a headache for a while but mostly it was a lot of boulder hopping. We were rewarded, though, by finding a few beers and sodas. Around 1600 we reached the sand and rock bar at Forster Rapids and made camp. It is possible to get from 128 Mile to Blacktail in one day, but we didn't want to move that fast.

*Route to Forster Rapids*

The night we spent at Forster Rapids is memorable for two reasons. It was the night we discovered a revolutionary new way for the Park Service to make money and it was the night I won my engineering battle with the ringtails but lost the war.

There was a wintry feel to the air and we were in our sleeping bags even before it was dark. That's one of the problems with late fall hiking – you may spend 12 to 14 hours in the sack. That is too long and as we were lying there wide awake, we considered what we could do about it. One good idea was to get a coupon book from the Backcountry Office entitling you to shorter winter nights. But we decided that if and when the Park Service got around to issuing them, they would be too expensive and, after all, the long nights would not be so tiresome if you could have a campfire.

*"Cheery* Then the lightbulb went on over our heads. All we had to
*Little* do was get the Park Service to sell a book of coupons, each
*Fire"* entitling the bearer to a "cheery little fire" – CLF for short.
*Coupons* After lengthy discussion we decided that, to prevent hoard-
ing and scalping, these coupons would have to be dated and
non-transferable. There would be one coupon for each night
of inner canyon camping and a book of five would cost
$5.00. A notation on the Backcountry Office copy of the
permit would show these coupons had been purchased, so
the Park Service would not necessarily have to react to every
fire it saw.

A year later I described this CLF coupon idea to a Park
Superintendent friend of my brother's as if it were fact. He
got more and more agitated the further I got in my story.
Finally, he interrupted and explained such an idea was
impossible – there was no way monies collected in that
fashion could get into the general coffers, and the fellows at
the Backcountry Ranger Office who sold me the coupons
had a scam going. He remained agitated long after I told him
I had made up the whole story.

*Outwitting* Fantasizing about CLF coupons is a right brain activity.
*the* Dealing with cacomistles is strictly left brain. We knew we
*Ringtail* were in for trouble from the very beginning. The campsite
we had chosen was covered with "wee beastie" tracks. I was
sure they were cacomistle tracks – too big for mice and too
small for other worse things. For the uninitiated, a cacomistle
is a relative of the raccoon. It is half tail, looks like a weasel
and is commonly called a "ringtailed cat." The Time/Life
book of the Grand Canyon calls it " . . . beautiful, intelligent,
playful and sometimes even affectionate." That may be, but
the book forgot to use the additional word "omnivorous."
But I knew that from previous encounters. Over the years I
have unintentionally fed them enough to have bought all
available affection. But I have none for them; they are pests
that rob you blind.

Knowing ringtails were about, I cantilevered my skipole
walking stick out from a chest high boulder as far as I could
get it by putting a large rock on the thick end and wedging
smaller ones in under the pole to bring the thin end farther
off the ground. Unfortunately, the rocks were well rounded
and my construction was barely stable – yet it seemed
servicable. I hung my food from the end of the pole. Both
Mattox and Benson had seen the trouble I had with the

construction and bet it wouldn't last the night. During the night I had several opprotunities to check on my skipole and all was well. My main problem came in protecting my fruit cocktail.

Usually I put the dehydrated fragments in my cup, add water and cover with a flat rock. Tonight, anticipating trouble, I inverted our cook pot over the cup and put the flat rock on top of the pot. Around midnight there was a rustling and rattling around the pot and eventually I was wrenched from my sleep to check it out. I was afraid whatever was about would push the pot around enough so the rock would fall off, or the cup would upset under the pot or perhaps both pot and cup would fall off the big rock they were on.

Checking things out with my flashlight, I found myself face-to-face with a ringtail. Without my glasses I have to get quite close to whatever I'm looking at to see it, so our heads were no more than 20 inches apart – the ringtail pushing on one side of the pot and me holding the other. I tried to scare it with something mild like "scat" but it wasn't the least bit intimidated. It made its chittering chipmunk noise and looked angry. Finally I let loose with a multi-decibel "shoo" that woke both Don and Robert and with a final snarl this affectionate beast left me alone for the rest of the night.

*Ringtail*
*Faceoff*

The next morning everything was exactly as it should be. My fruit cocktail was untouched and my food bags still hung from the end of the walking stick. Everything was intact, that is, except my food. It was hanging some distance from my sleeping bag and since I had taken my breakfast out the night before, I didn't check it carefully until we were packing up. Then I discovered that these "beautiful, intelligent, affectionate" creatures had foiled me again.

They had jumped up from below – about three feet – hung on by their front claws and chinned themselves up to where they could chew through the lowest food bag. This simple act rewarded them with a shower of powdered milk, cereal, noodles and jerky. The frenzy of footprints in what remained of the stuff that fell on them outlined the drama through which I had slept.

A thought just occurred to me – perhaps the ringtail who attacked my fruit cocktail was only a diversion to distract me from what the rest of the troops were doing. Of course, they didn't get all my food so I still had much better than starvation rations ahead of me. But I had lost something more precious than food – my pride.

*Long* Our sleeping bags were so wet with dew the next morning
*Tapeats* that we waited for the sun which, luckily, hit us early. The
*Sidewalks* going was easy. We climbed up on a Tapeats ledge for a
while and then dropped back down just before 122 Mile
Canyon. Both Fossil and Forster Rapids had long Tapeats
ledges at water level that are like sidewalks with watery
mouths snapping at you from the gutter.

*Blacktail* In Conquistador Aisle we climbed with the rising Tapeats
*Canyon* and again picked up a burro trail that made travel easy and
fast and we had lunch on the beach at Blacktail Canyon. We
climbed down the nose on the downstream side of the
canyon. Water was flowing at the mouth but not up in the
drainage above the chockstone. The same was true in 1982
and 1988. We explored a little and then had an early dinner
before pushing on a mile or so.

Although we thought we could get down to the River at
Explorers Monument, we weren't sure, and since the time
to our next water was uncertain, we wanted to shorten
tomorrow's run. The route back to the Tonto is up a series
of ledges about a hundred yards upriver from the mouth of
Blacktail.

The Tonto rises in two steps as you go south from Blacktail.
Two faults cross the river here – the Monument Fold. At the
southernmost of these faults we got a dramatic view of
folded Tapeats on the other side. The going got much more
difficult as we climbed and remained so until we were
opposite Elves Chasm. In 1988, however, we discovered a
burro trail close to the edge of the lowest cliff. We found no
water until we came to a small sad grungy pool in the
drainage at Explorers Monument.

*Route* We did, indeed, find a way off the Tonto to the river in a
*to* notch just west of the main drainage – between the "L" and
*River* the second "O" in "COLORADO." There is a little Tapeats
to go through, but the talus rises a long way to meet it. But,
having watched chocolate syrup flowing by for the last two
days, we decided that the sad grungy water we had was no
worse than the sad grungy water we could get. So we
strained out the dead bugs and made do.

While Don and I rested in the heat of the afternoon, Robert
tried to climb the Redwall via the Monument Fault ravine.
The crumbly cliffs stopped him, though, and he returned
disappointed. Later in the afternoon, as the shadows lengthened, we hiked on around the bend for about a half mile.

Here we made a dry camp, used the rest of our good water and boiled the smelly stuff we had brought with us from Explorers Monument.

We started early the next day. Don promised us a hot dry day, and he wanted to hike as much as possible in the cool of early morning. In about 15 minutes we crossed a flowing stream. We dumped the bad stuff and filled up with the good stuff, trying not to think of how much nicer a camp we would have had if we had just hiked a few more minutes the evening before. Oh well, that's life. *Good Flowing Water*

This water was also flowing the next October as well as in June 1988 and there was burro scat around so it is probably dependable. The existence of this spring makes this loop do-able in hot weather and it is so crucial I call it "Key Spring." However, the last two times I camped there I remember a subsequent day-long bout with diarrhea and since we had treated our water with iodine and Clorox in one case and filtered it in another, I am sure the problem is chemical. I do not remember what happened in 1981. Because of the possibility of having to retrace your steps to the River access point near Explorers Monument if Key Spring is dry, I recommend trying to find this access point as you pass it.

The rest of the day was as Don promised. In and out and up and down. But a burro trail helped enormously. The biggest pain was Waltenburg Canyon. It seemed to go on forever. We spent three hours in getting from the downstream point to the upstream one – a distance of less than half a River mile. The ramp into Hakatai Canyon was a little hard to find from the top but within a half hour we had found it and were heading down to water. We found it by going down the east side of a small cleft about 100 yards above the third "a" in "Hakatai Rapids." We had planned to camp at Shinumo Creek but since there was flowing water in Hakatai we decided to stay there. I went down to the River, Robert went upcanyon to try to find the end of Bass' trail and Don took a nap. *Good Burro Trail*

Even in 1982 there was quite a bit of memorabilia still left in Hakatai – tent platforms, cooking stuff, and of course, mining stuff. By 1988 the tent platforms were gone. The mines near our camp were very small, though it is conceivable that gravel has filled them up to some extent. Near the mouth of the creek you can climb up to a saddle overlooking the River *Hakatai Bass Camp* where the old cable was anchored, and Robert found the Hakatai end of the Bass trail almost at the upper end of the drainage. At first he thought it was a burro trail but as he followed it he found evidence of trail construction.

*Route to Burro Canyon* The next day we declined to use the trail Robert had found and instead took the familiar ravine more or less in line with the ramp we used to enter Hakatai. There is only one obstacle: a large chockstone. Coming on it from below we felt sure we could climb it with our packs on – that is, until we tried. But it is easier to climb up than down. After this it was smooth sailing over to Burro Canyon. The route into Burro is down a small ramp under a cliff and along a wide place between the 3360- and 3440-foot contours about 0.7 miles southeast of Fan Island. As you turn the corner to head north before descending to the bed of Burro, you may intersect the east end of Bass' Hakatai trail. Our trail continued on across Burro Canyon, up a ramp and around and down into Shinumo Creek.

*Bass Camp Historical Site* After we crossed the creek to the east side, it was only 15 minutes or so to Bass Camp Historical Site. For information about Bass and Bass Camp see the Tuna Creek/Shinumo Creek Loop chapter. We had lunch on the Shinumo Quartzite slabs just upstream from Bass Camp. There is plenty of water for a cooling dip if you don't mind minnows nibbling your toes.

*Route to Tapeats Spring* It is an easy and beautiful three hours from these Quartzite slabs up Shinumo Creek to White Creek and up White to the Tapeats narrows and a lovely spring. I often camp on the Tapeats slickrock above the chockstone at the spring, and Don and I and Robert did this time, too. Muav Canyon (White Creek flows in Muav Canyon) was dry above the chockstone, but water reappeared near the top of the Tapeats. It also reappeared in the Muav at the top of an extensive, though unnecessary, bypass where an overhanging rock and smooth Muav ledges can provide good camping. By this time our route had joined the North Bass Trail and two hours after we left the Tapeats spring, we reached the bottom of the Redwall climb – well used and marked. Harvey Butchart calls this a "surprising" Redwall route and indeed it is. Fortunately, in this case "surprising" doesn't mean "difficult". On top, the route crosses three drainages from the west before dropping back into Muav Canyon. A well marked, though brushy, trail leads across these drainages now.

For the next mile or so we followed the creek to the 5691 Benchmark. The North Bass Trail, now a well-beaten path, leaves the drainage at a spot where a log has been placed across the drainage. You will have passed other logs similarly placed so be observant. The Trail climbs steeply up the Hermit Shale to the base of the Coconino. Eventually we reached the main route that contours along the top of the shale to Muav Saddle. A little to the south on this trail there is a mapped spring that can be useful if you are hurting for water.

*Route to Muav Saddle*

A few hundred yards more and we were once again on Muav Saddle, having successfully concluded our circumambulation of Powell Plateau. All it all, it was easier than I expected – quite easy, I would say. Another 45-minute climb up the trail and we were at the car – a seven hour trip from the Tapeats chockstone. I remember hoping the car would start.

*Back to Swamp Point*

# — 5 —

# *TAPEATS CREEK*
# *KANAB CREEK*
# *LOOP*

An expression of the feeling of gratitude at seeing the approaching end of a difficult hike:
*"All's well that ends."*

Jim Hickerson

|  |  |
|---|---|
| *LENGTH* | 6 days, plus layover day(s), if any. |
| *WATER* | Fairly reliable spring at Redwall/Supai contact for trip down. Ample water in lower Indian Hollow drainage for trip out. |
| *QUAD MAPS (15')* | Jumpup Canyon, Arizona<br>Kanab Point, Arizona<br>Powell Plateau, Arizona |
| *ROADHEAD* | Indian Hollow Campground |
| *ROUTE TO ROADHEAD* | a) via Jacob Lake, Arizona. Go south from Jacob Lake on Highway 67 toward the North Rim 0.2 miles and turn right on Forest Service (FS) Road 461. In 1988 there was a new blue and white sign here with an arrow saying "Camping." After the turn you will see a sign saying "Big Springs 16." Be careful, though, to avoid the service road that turns off about 100 yards before the one you want. In what follows it is assumed that you have just turned off Highway 67 onto FS 461. |

After 4.3 miles, turn left at a fork and down a steep hill.

After 0.9 miles you meet FS 462 and turn right. It is now 10 miles to Big Springs.

After 3.0 miles you meet FS 422 from Fredonia and turn left.

After 6.4 miles you pass Big Springs Ranger Station.

After 4.8 miles turn right on FS 425. You will now see a sign saying "Thunder River Trailhead 10".

After 8.1 miles turn right on FS 232. A sign reads "Indian Hollow Campground 5".

After 5.0 miles you reach the end of the road about .25 miles beyond the campground.

The total time from Jacob Lake is 1:00 to 1:15 hours and the total distance is 32.7 miles.

b) via Fredonia, Arizona. Turn right on FS 422 just outside Fredonia on the way to Jacob Lake.

After about 22 miles you meet FS 462. Go straight on FS 422.

After passing this intersection, proceed as described above.

I hiked this loop in each direction in the fall of 1984 and collected the two sets of times shown in the following table. You can see that sometimes they are quite different. This difference is due principally to the fact that one trip was made in hot weather and the other in cool weather. The hot weather hike went to Kanab Creek first and the cool weather hike went to Deer Creek first. Reststops are self-perpetuating when it is hot and self-limiting when it is cold. Also, hiking times are lengthened considerably in hot weather because of time spent dunking in cooling pools found along the way. *TWO SETS OF HIKING TIMES*

| | | Hiking Times Between Locations | | |
|---|---|---|---|---|
| Use Areas | Locations | Cool | Hot | *HIKING TIMES* |
| ∆ Outside Park | Car | | | |
| | | 1:45 | 2:15 | |
| ∆ Fishtail | Ghost Rock | | | |
| | | :45 | 1:30 | |
| ∆ Fishtail | Cranberry Spring | | | |
| | | 1:00 | 1:15 | |
| ∆ Fishtail | Point Overlooking River | | | |
| | | 1:30 | 1:30 | |
| | Base of Talus | | | |
| | | 1:00 | 1:15 | |
| ∆ Deer Creek | Deer Creek Campsite | | | |
| | | :15 | :30 | |
| | Deer Creek Falls | | | |
| | | 1:45 | 1:45 | |
| | Siesta Spring | | | |

| | | | |
|---|---|---|---|
| | | Siesta Spring | |
| | | | 1:15 · 1:00 |
| Δ | Fishtail | Fishtail Canyon | |
| | | | 3:45 · 5:00 |
| Δ | Kanab Creek | Mouth of Kanab Canyon | |
| | | | 3:00 · 3:30 |
| | | Slide of Susurrus | |
| | | | 3:00 · 4:15 |
| Δ | Kanab Creek | Scotty's Hollow | |
| | | | :45 · 1:00 |
| Δ | Kanab Creek | Overhanging Spring | |
| | | | 3:00 · 3:15 |
| Δ | Kanab Creek | Jumpup/Kanab Confluence | |
| | | | 1:15 · 1:45 |
| | | Indian Hollow/Jumpup Confluence | |
| | | | :15 · :15 |
| | | Obstacle Pool* | |
| | | | :45 · 1:00 |
| Δ | Kanab Creek | Big Pool Camp | |
| | | | 3:30 · 4:00 |
| | | Base of Coconino | |
| | | | :30 · :45 |
| | | Top of Coconino | |
| | | | 2:00 · 2:00 |
| Δ | Outside Park | Car | |

* Time to Obstacle Pool does not include time to pass it which will be from thirty minutes to an hour depending on size of pool and size of party.

**ROUTE DETAILS** This loop takes you to three of the "must see" areas of Grand Canyon National Park: Tapeats Creek, with the fascinating waterworks at Thunder River, Deer Creek, with the deep narrow gorge and beautiful falls, and Kanab Canyon, with the 1,200-foot walls and scenic delights like Scotty's Hollow and the Slide of Susurrus.

I think of this loop as taking seven days but it could be done by fast hikers in six or even blitzed in five. To maximize pleasure I recommend the seven days or even eight or nine. The extra day(s) can be spent camping at Tapeats Creek or exploring the upper reaches of Deer Creek or Scotty's Hollow.

I will describe this loop as going to Deer Creek first because I think this is the easier way. Even though it means a long day, I recommend the extra effort required to get to Deer Creek the first day because that is where the assured water is. But three good places are shown on the map if you decide to camp enroute. Usually the hike to Deer Creek requires about six hours, including rest stops but not lunch, and in that time you will travel about seven miles and descend about 3,000 feet.

It is about a five-minute walk along the trail from car to rim, and I am never quite prepared for the suddenness of the view. If you have camped at your car, this will be the first verification of the facts that: 1) you are in the right place and 2) the canyon is still there. A great deal of your route can be seen from the rim so try to identify the 40-foot high east facing overhang called "Ghost Rock" and the drainage you will take to get down to the top of the Redwall.

*Rim Takeoff*

The trail, which is the original horse trail to Thunder River, angles down through the limestone and contours west along the top of the Toroweap Limestone for about a half mile to a break. Follow the zigzags of the trail down through the Coconino until you can angle down and west to a small red knoll of Hermit Shale. Keep angling down and west until you can find a convenient gully to take you down to the top of the Supai Formation. This broad expanse is called The Esplanade.

*Ghost Rock*

I can't place Ghost Rock on the map exactly, but I think it is either at or near the small sock-shaped bit of 4800-foot contour, with a benchmark of 4807 feet, about 0.9 miles below the "S" in the word "FOREST" on the quad map. You won't find any water at Ghost Rock unless rainfall has collected in pools on the Supai, but it is still a good place to camp.

*Cowboys and Indians*

Ghost Rock provides a small terrace protected by the over-hang where people seeking shelter have camped over the years. Except for the large "ghostly" figures painted on the east-facing wall and a small metate, I have seen no evidence of Indian occupancy. There is, however, a great deal of evidence of cowboy occupancy – storage cans, a horseshoe and fragments of leather tack. Possibly the pockmarks left by bullets fired at the ghost figures can be attributed to them as well.

From the late 1800s until only recently, ranchers brought their cattle down to the Esplanade on one of the several trails connecting it with the rim and left them there to graze during the summer. The remnants of these constructed trails can still be seen. They also built other trails so they could take their horses down from the Esplanade to graze on the top of the Redwall. Good examples of both can be found in 150 Mile Canyon.

There are other cowboy camps on the Esplanade besides the one at Ghost Rock – one between Kanab Canyon and 150 Mile Canyon and one between 150 Mile Canyon and Tuckup Canyon. The latter camp is under a large overhang covered on its underside with elaborate pictographs.

To continue on to Deer Creek you go south, working your way down through the upper Supai layers, to the head of a drainage leading down to the canyon between Fishtail Canyon and Deer Creek. It is unnamed on the map, but Harvey Butchart credits David Mortenson with giving it the name "Cranberry Canyon" when, on Thanksgiving Day, Mortenson first used this route to get to Deer Creek.

*Cranberry* Cranberry Canyon is an expression of the Sinyala Fault which
*Canyon* extends southwest across the Colorado River even beyond Havasu Creek. The fault also continues northeast across Deer Creek. There are two fault ravines leading down to Cranberry Canyon. I use the western one because it is closer. You will find a small, dripping spring behind a big boulder just below where the two fault ravines meet at the Redwall/Supai contact. This spring has provided me with water every time I have been there – one time in summer and four times in fall – and gives a quart of water in about ten minutes. In 1988 we also found water by a redbud on the Redwall in some heavy greenery on the west side of Cranberry.

Continue on down the drainage from the spring until it is convenient to climb up to the east onto the broad terrace lying on top of the Redwall. It is easy going out to the point overlooking the Colorado River. This point is also a good place to camp. There is no water but there is a great view.

The Redwall Limestone forms an imposing cliff and, in spite of the thousands of miles of Redwall in the Canyon, there are very few breaks in it where a hiker can get through. Like the descent to Deer Creek, the great majority of these breaks are along faults. Continue east from the overlook at the mouth of Cranberry along the top of the Redwall for about a half mile to the sharp bend in the Supai wall about 0.2 miles west of the 4670' benchmark. The chute you want goes down steeply in a series of steps that unfortunately blocks the view of where you want to go so you may think you are off route. Once this happened to me and I went on to the next chute which looked even worse. The second time around the correct chute looked much better.

The chute is narrow and steep, but no rope is needed unless you want one for lowering packs. Be very careful to avoid knocking rocks loose. If you do, yell *"rock"* as loudly as you can so those below you have some time to get out of the way. A series of steep pitches, amounting to a 100 feet or so, leads to a dropoff and here you must contour around to the right (west) for 50 yards or so to the top of a big talus slope. Go down it carefully because the whole slope seems above the angle of repose. But if you think the talus slope is steep, try looking over the eastern edge. There the rubble forms an almost vertical cliff. It looks scary.

*Redwall Break*

Descend until you can cross the drainage safely near the 3700-foot contour a little above the dry lake bed to the east. A word about crossing drainages cut deeply into rubble. *Do not* attempt to climb up or down them. Instead, contour in and out, stepping very carefully on the smaller boulders.

Contour around and down to the dry lake bed and go over a saddle to the south. It is tempting to go over a lower saddle to the east, but it leads to steep terrain that is tedious to climb through. After crossing the higher saddle, pick your way down the other side to the flats 300 feet below and then turn east and work your way down the hillside to Deer Creek. When you get to the creek you will be near the spot where it cuts through the Tapeats Sandstone to enter the narrows. According to the Grand Canyon National Park Backcountry Management Plan, you are permitted to camp anywhere here as long as it is upstream from the "upper end of the narrows."

Unfortunately, I must caution you to purify the Deer Creek water as several people I know, including me, have become sick after drinking it. In the summer, inconsiderate hikers and visitors from boat parties bathe and wash their hair in the creek. As a result there is considerable soapy pollution and fecal contamination of the stream. There is less bathing in Tapeats Creek because it is colder, but I would purify that water, too.

*Purify Water*

The water for Deer Creek comes from two springs. One is in the main bed about a half mile from the upper end of the narrows and the other, called Deer Spring on the quad map, forms a fall in the cliff on the western edge of Surprise Valley. Coming from Surprise Valley by trail you can hear these falls long before you get a chance to see them. The

*Deer Creek*

trail has now been rerouted to pass near the falls and there is a short spur trail to them.

*Roundtrip to Tapeats Creek* If you have the time for it, I certainly recommend the nine-hour hike to Thunder River and Tapeats Creek and back. But should you wish to camp over there and spend more time exploring, be advised that Tapeats Creek is a Designated Site Use Area. This means camping is restricted to specific sites; namely, to the Upper and Lower Designated Sites. You should request permission for use of one of these campsites when you apply for your permit. The Upper Sites are distributed along the west side of Tapeats Creek downstream from its confluence with Thunder River and the Lower Sites are on the beaches by the Colorado River. In addition, the whole Thunder River drainage, from Tapeats Creek to the lip of Surprise Valley, is closed to camping.

*Route to Tapeats Creek* The route to Tapeats Creek through Surprise Valley begins with the trail up the west side of Deer Creek, which crosses the creek under some huge cottonwoods by an inviting pool. After crossing, you follow the trail up through the rocks to the lip of Surprise Valley. You pass the spur trail to the fall at Deer Spring, which is the last water until you get to Thunder River in about two hours.

*Surprise Valley* The trip through Surprise Valley is mainly uphill and, unless you get an early start, *hot* in the summer months – May through September. Once, on a summer's afternoon, I urgently needed something with which to dig a cat hole and unwisely picked up a dark piece of rock. I blistered all the fingers that touched that rock. My thermometer read 135°F at ground level but, fortunately, only 95°F waist high. But it isn't always hot in Surprise Valley. Once we hiked through with our boots going squish, squish, squish. An extensive thunderstorm had dumped an inch of water over the whole valley in just a few minutes.

*Slump* Surprise Valley, and the smaller valley and dry lake bed that you crossed earlier in getting to Deer Creek, represent a spectacular geological event. According to Ford, Huntoon, Billingsley and Breed (see the article "Rock movement and mass wastage in the Grand Canyon" from the book *Geology of the Grand Canyon*), they are the result of a huge rotational landslide or slump. Visualize a segment of canyon wall, from the Bright Angel Shale on the bottom to the Esplanade on the top, which is ½ to 1½ miles wide and 2,000 feet thick, extending from Thunder River on the east to Cranberry Canyon on the west. Suddenly this hunk of wall slips on the shale, breaks loose from its moorings and rotates with the bottom portion moving out and away as the top portion falls. It is possible that the shale was lubricated by water backed up behind the lava dams farther downstream. In any case, this huge landslide dammed the Colorado River at a point just below Deer Creek which you can see on your way to Kanab Canyon.

The results of the slump are very visible in Surprise Valley. For example, you may have sought shade behind great Supai boulders that are about 1,500 feet below their former neighbors on the Esplanade. And off to the north, near where the Thunder River trail heads up to the Supai rimrock, you can see segments of Redwall with their Esplanade caps below and tilted toward the cliff from which they slumped.

Coming from the oven of Surprise Valley, you find a startling contrast at Thunder River. Besides being the shortest river in the world – it is a half mile long – it also has the dubious distinction of being the only river in the world that flows into a creek. But whatever it is, it is cold. Standing in the shade where the downdraft of the falls blows a strong wind of evaporatively cooled spray on you, you can feel *freezing*.

*Thunder River*

Such a luxuriance of water seems out of place – a most wonderful contradiction – and it is easy to shoot a whole roll of film of just water. Water in many forms – running water, falling water, spraying water, dripping water, white foaming water, dark calm water; they are all there. It is possible to climb up to the opening from which the majority of the water flows, and, indeed, spelunkers have mapped thousands of feet of cave, but it is a dangerous climb and I don't recommend it. There is considerable exposure and it is certainly not for the acrophobic. For those who are so inclined a special permit, obtained from the Resource Management people, is required for any cave exploration in the Park.

It is less than a mile on a good trail from Thunder Springs to Tapeats Creek and the upper campsites.

Sometime in 1983 or 84, the Park Service installed a solar-powered privy at the Upper Tapeats Creek campsites; so don't be surprised when you see the solar cells. The idea is to power a small fan to dehydrate the contents of the holding tank so a helicopter won't have to come in as often to replace the tank.

*Tapeats Creek*

Just below the southernmost campsite, the main trail crosses the creek. It crosses back about two miles on down. However, if your trip is during high water in spring or early summer, when the flow is so steep and fast you might lose your footing and never recover it, there is another route, less used and more up and down, that stays entirely on the west side. To minimize "multiple trailing", it should be used only when it is dangerous to cross the creek.

Not far above the place where the trail crosses the creek the second time, the water pours into a narrow slot in the red shale. This creates a U-shaped fall that makes a real cauldron of frothy water. If you sit on the edge and watch the fall carefully, you, like Mattox, may be rewarded by seeing a very large trout trying to jump it.

It was also near here that I saw my first hyperthermia victim and I am going to describe the incident because the condition, though not common, is so very possible and at the same time so dangerous.

*Heatstroke Victim* The young man in question, about 18 or 19, well built and athletic, was a member of a small group of nudists that I first saw dunking themselves in Deer Creek on a hot afternoon in August. They had just come from Monument Point through the oven of Surprise Valley so their nudity in the water was most natural and I thought nothing of it. But, later, when they came through camp I could see it was no ordinary group. The leader asked about the route along the Colorado River upstream to Tapeats Creek and I described it as best I could and told him we would also be going that way the next morning and they could follow us. He went off and they camped above us on a knoll.

The next morning we passed them as they were having breakfast. In midmorning as we were resting before taking the ramp down to the River, I saw them high up above us contouring around among the cliffs. This must have been very hot and slow and they were wearing nothing but their boots – not even a hat. The next evening we were camped near Thunder River and the leader appeared and said one of his party was sick with an upset stomach and asked whether I had any appropriate medication. He suspected bad water. I said I didn't and he left.

The next noon when we were playing in the cauldron by the U-shaped falls, the leader appeared again saying the young man was worse, still couldn't keep any food down and had chills and would I take a look at him. They were all in clothes by this time. I did look at him but couldn't offer a diagnosis. He was shivering, though, and wanted a blanket. But he did seem to be hot and his friends were trying to cool him off. They finally used a signal mirror to call for help and within an hour a helicopter was there. The paramedic checked the pulse (a little fast but not much) and checked the armpits for sweat (there was none). But not sweating is a critical part of the diagnosis of hyperthermia and the helicopter took the young man to the clinic on the South Rim and that was the last I saw of him.

A year or so later, when I was in their part of the country, I called the man who had been their leader to find out what had happened to the young man. He told me it had been hyperthermia and that when the doctor couldn't stablize him at the clinic, he had been transferred to intensive care in the hospital at Flagstaff. The doctors there worked on him for a week before his core temperature returned to normal and stayed that way. He had nearly died and would have to be very careful of heat for the rest of his life.

What I didn't know then about hyperthermia and the reason I have described an occurrence of it at such length is that it is so easy to misread the symptoms.

How can the victim's sensation be one of cold when he is overdosing on heat? The answer is that usually the blood is in the capillaries near the surface trying to give up heat to the sweating exterior, but shutdown occurs when the body can't get rid of the heat fast enough and gives up and says "why bother." The capillaries are shut down, the blood withdrawn to the core and the patient's sensation is one of cold.

That ends the digression. But remember, if you see someone in the heat of summer who feels cold and who is not sweating, get help immediately because that person may be near death.

Many inviting pools lurk in the lower part of Tapeats Creek. Some have "swim in me" signs so allow time to oblige. When the diabase sill with its Bass Formation cap emerges, the trail follows the ramp up and around to a break where there is a quick drop to the beach below. A trail going up the corresponding ramp on the east side ends up at Stone Creek.

*Route to Stone Creek*

The route back to Deer Creek continues downstream at River level to Bonita Creek. At high water you will get "cliffed out" and must go up and over a basalt shoulder that extends out into the water. At low water, you can go around near the water, but be careful. The handholds are good but the polished wet rock can be very slippery. Again, it is a good idea to undo your waistband while making this traverse.

You have a choice of routes when you reach the drainage about 1.2 miles past Bonita Creek. One is to follow the ramp in the Bass Formation capping the emerging schist. The River is very narrow here – one book says it narrows to 35 feet. I like this ramp. The going is easy and overhangs provide shelter or shade as needed. The other choice is to take the steep route straight up to the top of the Tapeats and contour around and up to the small saddle mentioned below.

*Grand Canyon Supergroup* The ramp and the strata above it are members of a formation called the Grand Canyon Supergroup. These Precambrian rocks are the oldest sedimentary rocks in the canyon and between them and the bottom of the Tapeats there is about 800 million years of geology missing. The Supergroup is visible only occasionally in the Canyon so its appearance is always interesting.

After you have topped out the ramp, you will soon cross a small wash and begin climbing up to a small saddle just south and east of the contour designation "2400" on the quad map. From there it is an easy drop back to camp.

If you happen to be going the other way through here on your way upstream to Tapeats Creek, you have your choice of routes as soon as you start down from the small saddle. What appears to be the better trail (in 1988) takes you over to the steep descent to the beach. This is probably the way the nudists were going when I saw them high above me. If you want to find the ramp, you have to cross the good trail and continue on down to another trail you will find below you.

I have been to Deer Creek more often than I have been to any other place in the Canyon, not because it is my favorite, though it is one of them, but because it is so easy to get to – only a long half day off Monument Point. It is also a friendly place. I especially like lying on the smooth warm rock like a lizard – after the shade has come – and listening to the different sounds the water is making. Sometimes you also hear the water ouzel and the canyon wren making their distinctive calls.

And don't forget the jacuzzi. Just before Deer Creek drops into the gorge, there is a place where its swirling action has excavated a bathtub-sized hole about three feet deep. This is the jacuzzi, and to prepare it for use you may wish to spend some time removing the cobbles from the otherwise smooth bottom of the tub. Then you can brace your feet against the downstream lip and submerge yourself for some pounding in the rushing turbulence.

*Jacuzzi*

But there are many things to do besides stretching out on the warm rocks like a lizard. Going up Deer Creek Canyon makes an interesting day. But take enough water; I have learned from experience that a quart is not enough. It is pretty easy going until you get past the spring a ways. After that you encounter gigantic rocks piled in the canyon wall to wall that are a challenge to climb through. Eventually this jumble, which probably resulted from the same slumping action that filled Surprise Valley, is behind you and the canyon forks.

*Upper Deer Creek Canyon*

If you go straight ahead, the Redwall narrows until only a slot remains and you have to swim in yucky water if you want to go any farther. I always give up at this point so I don't know if the route goes or not. If you go east at the fork, you will eventually dead end at a 100-foot dryfall in a big amphitheater. There is a way to climb up on the north to the top of the dryfall, and my brother and I were going up easily (his word, not mine) until I strongly suggested ("demanded" is a better word) we go back. He is a good climber but I needed either a belay or a net.

Exploring this canyon is very rewarding, and the climb through the jumble very strenuous – all in all a typical activity for a rest day.

For the more sedentary I recommend the waterfall at Deer Spring for the morning, the big fall by the Colorado River for midday and the gorge for the afternoon. The gorge comes last because only the midafternoon sun shines down there and that makes for better pictures. Also save some time in the late afternoon for enjoying the jacuzzi.

The entry to the gorge is off a shoulder just below the first chockstone on the opposite side of the gorge from the trail. It is easy to get down the ledges to a small rounded buttress but getting down that buttress is harder. It can be done free if you trust your friction, but it is psychologically helpful to have a rope to hold onto even if you don't need it.

*Deer Creek Gorge*

As you go down the stream you will pass an alcove that harbors a small redbud tree struggling to hang on to life through the flash floods. It must surely be the most photographed tree in the Park below the rim. A little farther and you come to a chockstone with about a 20-foot pouroff. I have anchored a rope here and climbed down beside the fall, but another chockstone, this one with a 90-foot pouroff, comes so soon after the first as to make the first descent a waste of time. There are, however, pitons at the pouroff, so someone has gone on a bit farther, at least.

If you value your life, it is best not to be in the gorge when there is the threat of a thunderstorm. Flash floods do happen here. Sometime about 10 years ago, a large segment of the west wall fell onto the Tapeats slickrock, completely burying the rocky beauty of the place – including my lizarding rocks and the jacuzzi – under tons of rubble. I visited Deer Creek twice while it looked like that and heaved great quantities of debris into the gorge trying to tidy up. I shouldn't have wasted my time, for a year or so later a flash flood came through and did the job for me – everything was shoved into the gorge. The bigger rocks didn't get beyond the first fall, so they form a pile of debris there while waiting for a bigger flood.

It is such a long day of boulder-hopping from Deer Creek to Kanab Creek that, after the first time, I have always split it into two half days. The first of the leftover half days can easily be spent at Deer Creek Falls.

*Indian Hand Prints* The way from camp to the bottom of Deer Creek Falls follows a well-defined trail along the west rim of the gorge. In some places the gorge is only about six feet wide at the top and I have been told that some river runners have jumped across in spite of the 50-foot penalty. As you go along this trail note the many whitish handprints, like spray painted outlines of hands, that are relics of the Indian occupancy. I hate to admit how many times I had been to Deer Creek before I saw them, and even then it was only because a ranger told me they were there. They are obvious in an odd way – when I didn't know they were there I never saw them, yet when I did know, I saw them in almost every likely spot. There are big ones, small ones, righthand ones, lefthand ones and even a few of leaves.

After you get out to the point where you can look down on the boats below, if there are any, the trail goes down steeply to the River. The point is also a good place to go for an after dinner stroll to watch the sunset or just to admire the view up past Tapeats Creek to Powell Plateau.

Like those at Thunder River, the falls here also create a strong downdraft that turns horizontal when it hits the pool, blasting you with icy air while you are trying to get up courage for a plunge into the cold water. Once, on a dare, I swam under the falls and came up behind them. I had a ledge to stand on and enough air to breathe but I was still frightened. This stunt was stupid because rocks go over the falls, too. *Deer Creek Falls*

It is an easy three hours down to Fishtail Canyon. As you proceed along the River, you almost get cliffed out by the Tapeats Sandstone about 0.8 miles downstream from the falls. Fortunately, there are ledges that make it possible to get by. The interesting thing (Ford, Huntoon, Billingsley and Breed, loc.cit.) about this bit of Tapeats is that it once was on the south side of the River. Before the slump I described earlier created a dam, the River flowed somewhere farther north, perhaps under the dry lake you crossed. The dam forced it to seek the new path it follows today.

Beyond the bend with these Tapeats ledges you come to a broad beach, and downstream beyond it you will see cliffs which stop you from continuing on down. A trail, which goes up and over the cliffs, leaves the beach to follow a draw going northeast about a mile downstream from the falls. Soon the trail leaves the draw and begins contouring around to Cranberry Canyon. Actually, there are several paths contouring around at different levels so don't be disturbed if you see one below you. Eventually they all converge.

A beautiful flow of water comes down one of the drainages you cross. It is such a delightful place for a siesta that I call it "Siesta Spring." Not far beyond the spring, the path descends to the Colorado River. Note the wall of cobblestones as you go down. The stones look river polished and may date from the time when the river was flowing farther north. After you reach the River, it is less than a half hour to the many possible campsites at Fishtail Canyon. *Siesta Spring*

It is a straightforward half day of boulder-hopping to get from Fishtail Canyon to Kanab Canyon and I would guess it is 90 percent boulders and 10 percent soft sand. It is surprising how much concentration is required to hike on a boulder field like this, and when it is hot, you will find there isn't much shade. Still, all things pass and after a while you will find yourself at Kanab Canyon. If the water is high, a sizeable estuary is formed where the water of the creek is "dammed" up by the River. If the River is not too high, you can wade to the other side where the good camping places are but, if you do, try it first without a pack to test the mud.

If you can't wade, take the high road. Begin by going north through the trees next to the cliff until you can scramble up to a path that goes along a ledge. Contour along above the creek until you can drop down to the cobbles below. Then cross and go back to the campsites on the other side.

*Route* | Actually, no routefinding is required; just head up the creek.
*to* It is an easy six-hour hike if you don't rest too much. But if
*Scotty's* it is summer, a few swims can add an hour or so, and
*Hollow* detouring to see The Slide of Susurrus can add another hour or so. But they are hours well spent. Two of the sights to see along the way are the long walkways on Muav ledges. One is long and the other is very long and they are both on the east side of the creek. These smooth ledges help make the Muav Limestone a "friendly" formation.

*Slide* But the Slide of Susurrus is the main attraction for today.
*of* It is a short distance up the major drainage that comes into
*Susurrus* the creek a little over three miles up from the mouth – about 0.4 miles north of the "C" in "Creek" on the quad map. The name, "Slide of Susurrus", is offered by my nephew. The slide is known by many names: "Whispering Falls", "Mystic Falls", "Ponce's Pond", "The Trogolyte Grotto". It is mystical; it is whispering; it is a grotto; it even has a pond of crystal clarity. But it is *not* a waterfall; it is definitely a slide. Well, maybe there is a little fall a foot high at the end of the slide and there are drips into the pool from high up, but I still maintain that it is not a fall. So "slide" is the right word. The word "susurrus" is an onomatopoetic word describing a rustling or whispering sound and suggests a much more mystical quality than "whispering". So "The Slide of Susurrus" it is, right? Oh well, I tried.

The Slide is much photographed – a challenge in itself – and I always sample the restorative powers of the pool through complete immersion. It is a place for reflection and the music of a recorder. A word of caution, though, for every beautiful apple can have its worm. This worm is the fact that this water, too, must be purified.

You can climb up to the ledge above the slide about a quarter mile upstream from the mouth of Slide Canyon and contour back and in. If you do, I'm told you will find a game trail, and where it crosses the water that forms the slide there is a mucky wallow and bushels of droppings. Well, so much for the crystal clarity of Ponce's Pond.

It is about three hours from the mouth of Slide Canyon to Scotty's Hollow. This name is suggested by the name "Scotty's Castle" already given to the tower that stands at the point where Kanab Creek does a 180-degree turn by the mouth of the side canyon. You can see from the quad map that there is a similar tower over a mile downstream so don't confuse the two. There is a fine cave to camp in during a storm, located on the south side of this false Scotty's Castle, a little downstream from the drainage that comes in from the west. The dryfall at the mouth of this side canyon sometimes provides a small dripping spring. Sometimes a deer trail goes up and over a neck of land formed by a sharp turn, although one has to look carefully to find it. *Scotty's Castle*

A good flow of water comes down Scotty's Hollow, but again I have to warn that it needs purification.

There are two things to do here on a layover day – explore the side canyon or climb the castle. I have never wanted to do the climb, though my brother and a friend did, so I spend my time exploring the Hollow. After the climb to get above the first fall, you find a series of pools strung in a cascade and farther on you find a polished limestone pavement connecting small bathtubs. *Scotty's Hollow*

About a mile and a half up the drainage, a side canyon comes in from the southwest that will take you through the Redwall and on up to the Esplanade if you so desire. This Redwall route is one of the few that is not on a fault, and a group I was with used it once to go from Kanab Canyon to 150 Mile Canyon.

Going up it is one thing and going down it is another. I was told by my friend Robert Benson, an experienced Canyon explorer, that it can be very difficult for a solo hiker to come down this arm when all its pools are full of water. On his first try Robert gave up trying to enter the steeply sloping upper ends of these deep pools with his heavy pack. Later he came back with a one man inflatable vinyl raft and made a successful descent. This route through the Redwall is a lot of fun without a pack, requiring, as it does, chimneying and layout traverses to avoid getting your feet wet.

Continuing from Scotty's Hollow to Indian Hollow is

another fun day with few challenges. Just remember to turn right at Jumpup Canyon and right again at Indian Hollow.

*Dripping Spring*  Near the "K" in "Kanab" you pass an overhanging spring. It is less than an hour from Scotty's and is certainly drinkable without treatment, at least I hope so. The creek has sharply undercut the bank that supports the spring and the spring in turn supports a luxuriant growth from which a sizeable flow of water rains down on the opposite shore. There are stretches of creek after the overhanging spring filled with Supai blocks, and the going is tiresome and tricky.

*Pencil Spring*  Another place, much closer to Jumpup Canyon, has a small pencil-sized stream of water squirting out near the bottom of a wall like a leak in a dike, and a few feet farther there is a good spring from which to refill your water bottles. There is no more good water until you are in Indian Hollow for a while. On occasion, Kanab Creek may be flowing past Jumpup, but it flows through cattle country so treat the water before drinking it.

*Kanab Spring Upstream Jumpup*  If you ever get to the Kanab/Jumpup junction badly in need of water, perhaps wanting to camp there, I have always found some about twenty minutes up Kanab Creek. Pass the first cleft on the left and enter the second. You will find water behind the chockstone; it is best to have two people in case one has to help the other over the chockstone. Sadly, graffiti now graces this quiet alcove. You may also be surprised, as I once was, to see jeep tracks here at Jumpup.

*Obstacle Pool*  As I said earlier, turn right into Jumpup Canyon and in a little more than an hour turn right again into Indian Hollow. About fifteen minutes after that, you encounter the fun part of the day. The first time I came through here, the obstacle was only a chockstone, and an easy one at that. Now it is a chockstone with a big pool, and until it changes back you have the choice of swimming or climbing. In September, I found the swims to be refreshing – I think I swam the pool at least ten times to bring all my stuff across. In November, swimming was out of the question, so climbing was the only way. Fortunately, we had eager climbers with us. But things change, and in October 1988 the pool was small enough to wade.

There is a route up the south wall by a small tree. One of us climbed up and belayed the rest. If there is no one in your party who wants to climb the wall without a belay, the only alternative is for a belayer to swim through the ice water and contour back above the rest. Even in summer this is not a bad idea. One person swims and hauls up all the packs, then the rest swim, but only once.

Not far above the obstacle the canyon narrows ominously, *Redwall* and sure enough there is another set of chockstones with a *Knife* big pool. This time, though, there is a bypass on the left. You go up a draw about 100 yards back and contour around until you can climb back down by the chockstones. Near the top of the draw there is a piece of Redwall that justifies my claim that the Redwall is "unfriendly." This chunk of limestone has a sharp knifelike crystal blade embedded in it. The blade is about two inches long, an inch high and an eighth-inch thick. If I had fallen on it, I would have been sliced open as neatly as with a razor blade.

There is a big over-your-head pool about an hour beyond the *Over* obstacle and it is a good place for a camp. It is also the only *Your* pool you will see beyond the chockstones in Indian Hollow *Head* that is deep enough in which to swim, and I did so even on *Pool* that cold November day.

The big pool is about at the top of the Redwall, and the next *Beautiful* few miles take you through the Supai. I am fond of Supai *Supai* gorges, especially if they have flowing water. Then they *Gorge* provide a peaceful mix of reds, blues and greens and reflections of all three. Small life forms are in abundance, cottonwoods flourish and, for the most part, the way is flat.

As you near the top of the Supai Formation it is important to keep track of where you are. Near the word "Indian" in "Indian Hollow" you will have four choices to make at a series of intersections, so be prepared. Eventually you leave the comfortable surroundings of the Supai and work up through rubble to the top of the Hermit Shale. Here the going gets rough as you climb up and around the huge boulders that block the way until you reach the maple glade that marks the bottom of the Coconino Sandstone. There will probably be a small trickle of water here and it is certainly a cool place for a rest.

The route through the Coconino is in three steps. The first *Coconino* step takes you up a cleft directly on your left as you face up *Clefts* the drainage. It is an easy climb, but the cleft is so narrow that your packs have to be hauled up. From here you contour around and up to a second cleft that is almost too narrow for packs. It is jammed with logs fitted into cracks so it would be very easy without a pack. This is the second step.

From the top of this cleft you work your way back into the drainage, fight some brush, and finally reach the final chockstone and the last step – a short ramp by a tree. If you don't like fighting with the tree you can crawl up under the chockstone – part of a tree branch is placed there to help you.

*Tedious Brush*  The brush is three to four feet high so it is helpful to have brought long pants because two hours of brush like this can remove some skin. This final part of the trip is tedious, and I often found myself thinking we were almost at the car long before we actually were.

When I get back to the car at the end of a trip it is time for refreshment, wine and cheese and crackers or beer or whatever, and it is also time for another important ritual. The shower. I always bring enough water for this treat and try to leave it in the car in such a position that it gets afternoon sun and is warm, hopefully hot, when I need it. I'm sure my companions on the ride home appreciate my shower as much as I.